BULLY FOR YOU, OSCAR

BULLY FOR YOU, OSCAR

OSCAR

*The Life and Times of a
Lancashire Cricket Legend*

**Ian Austin with
Andrew Collomosse**

MAINSTREAM
PUBLISHING

EDINBURGH AND LONDON

**TO MY FAMILY, WHO HAVE ALL SUPPORTED ME
SO MUCH IN SO MANY DIFFERENT WAYS.**

First published in Great Britain in 2000 by
MAINSTREAM PUBLISHING COMPANY (EDINBURGH) LTD
7 Albany Street
Edinburgh EH1 3UG

ISBN 1 84018 361 6

A catalogue record for this book is available from the British Library

Typeset in Berkeley Book and Triplex Condensed
Printed and bound by Butler and Tanner Ltd, Frome and London

CONTENTS

ACKNOWLEDGEMENTS

A special word of thanks to literally thousands of people who have backed me for so long. To everyone at Haslingden CC and all the other Lancashire League clubs who helped me in the early years. To my teammates at Lancashire. To all the Lancashire members, supporters, staff and officials for their support on and off the field. To John Cotton and everyone connected with my Benefit Year. To the press, radio and television who, by and large, have given me a fair crack of the whip. For this book, thank you to the *Lancashire Evening Telegraph*, Alan Shepherd, Phill Heywood, Paul Agnew PR and especially David and John Dawson of Cricketimages for allowing me to use their pictures. To Lancashire statistician Malcolm Lorimer for his facts and figures. To Mike Atherton for the foreword. And finally to Graham Knowles, once of Haslingden CC. I know you beat my record, Graham, and I'll make sure you get a mention in the credits when *Bully for you, Oscar* hits Hollywood!

THE CAST

It sometimes feels as if I've been involved with a million and one cricketers. Perhaps it isn't quite that many . . . but in 15 years on the Lancashire staff there have been a hell of a lot. And all my teammates have had a nickname, some more obscure than others. Here's a list of a few that you are likely to come across in the book, not necessarily in order of appearance:

IAN AUSTIN	Bully Oscar
ALAN ORMROD	Ormers
DAVID HUGHES	Yozzer, Hughesie
CLIVE LLOYD	Mr Lloyd, Sir
JACK SIMMONS	Simmo
DAVID LLOYD	Bumble
GRAEME FOWLER	Foxy
PAUL ALLOTT	Walt
JOHN ABRAHAMS	Abey
DEXTER FITTON	Dex
GEHAN MENDIS	Mendo
MIKE WATKINSON	Winker, Watky
NEIL FAIRBROTHER	Harvey
JOHN STANWORTH	Stanny
PHIL DEFREITAS	Daffy
WASIM AKRAM	Waz
MICHAEL ATHERTON	Athers
NICK SPEAK	Speaky, Judge

WARREN HEGG	Chucky
PETER MARTIN	Digger
GARY YATES	Yatesy, Sweaty
GRAHAM LLOYD	Bumble
GLENN CHAPPLE	Chappy, Boris
JOHN CRAWLEY	Creeps
MUTTIAH MURALITHARAN	Murali
ANDREW FLINTOFF	Fred, Flinty
MIKE SMETHURST	Smethers
GARY KEEDY	Keeds
CHRIS SCHOFIELD	Schoey
SOURAV GANGULY	Ravi

FOREWORD
BY MICHAEL ATHERTON

To put it simply, Ian Austin has been one of the best Lancashire cricketers of the last decade. We've had a lot of international players and high-class overseas men, but over the years Oscar has won a shedload of games for us. He's been a vital cog in the machine. People outside Lancashire might not appreciate that. But inside the county they all know about Oscar; that he's been an integral part of one of the most successful sides in one-day cricket. And hopefully there's a bit more to come. Oscar is a key man in dressing-room life, as well as being chairman/ secretary/ manager of our golf society. A vital job!

He's always been a sociable guy off the field. He has looked after himself a lot more as he's grown older – hence his lack of injury problems until the last couple of seasons – but in his formative years you could rely on him being first into the bar and last out. In fact, Oscar has a lot to answer for in that respect. He was the man who led me on my first excursion into the perils of the demon drink on a National Cricket Association tour of Bermuda back in 1985. I was 16, Oscar was a couple of years older, and it's fair to say that tour was quite an experience for us both. I'd played alongside him for the Lancashire Federation team earlier that year. There was a whole group of us who grew up together: Oscar, Warren Hegg, Dexter Fitton, Nick Speak, Graham Lloyd and me. We were always good mates, all the way into the Lancashire side. A close-knit group.

Bully initially made his name as a one-day specialist. He bowled straight, made useful runs and was usually around to drag us out of the mire when the batsmen failed. Those virtues have made him an important part of the Championship side. He might easily have played more international cricket. When he got the call in 1998 and went on to play in the World Cup the following year, he was maybe a little past his peak. His time was probably a bit earlier. But he's a much better player than many people give him credit for. It's easy for the away spectators not to take him seriously because of his build, but our fans love him and he has taken on Jack Simmons's mantle as the members' favourite. They idolise Oscar in the north of the county, his home territory, and I'm sure that when he calls it a day with Lancashire, he'll go back into the leagues and be a tremendous club professional.

Even though he led me astray all those years ago in Bermuda, I'm delighted to write this foreword. Bully for you, Oscar!

October 2000

PROLOGUE
WHO EATS ALL THE PIES? NOT ME!

Judge me on my figures, not my figure. That is all I ask. I've spent most of my career listening to taunts from supporters of 'Sumo, Sumo' and 'Who ate all the pies?' I've put up with newspapers relating half-truths about my eating and drinking habits. And I've learned to live with the reality that for some people my waistline is more important than my line and length.

Let's get one thing straight for starters. I don't spend the best part of my life eating meat pies and swilling down pints of ale. Never have done; never will. Unfortunately, because of the physique I was born with, I've had to put up with that reputation since I first started to make a name for myself, nearly 15 years ago. I'll give you an example. Lancashire played Gloucestershire at Bristol in a Benson & Hedges Cup semi-final at the end of last May. My Mum had been desperately ill, so I went into the game without having played any serious cricket for the best part of two weeks. I had to take the field knowing that Mum's funeral would take place 24 hours or so later – yet I still managed to produce figures of 10 overs, two maidens, 17 runs, no wickets. Despite this, the radio commentary team seemed, as usual, more concerned with my shape than my performance. 'You don't see many cricketers built like Austin in this era of 32-inch waistlines.' That kind of thing. Well, maybe you don't. But you don't get many cricketers who can bowl ten overs for 17 runs in a one-day semi-final either. Thankfully, David 'Syd' Lawrence, the former Gloucester bowler, was also in the box and pointed that out on my behalf. Thanks, pal!

I'm an easy target, I suppose. I can guarantee that as soon as I take my place on the boundary edge in a one-dayer, the chants of 'Who ate all the pies?' and 'Sumo' will start – mostly from opposing fans with several pies and pints already on board, and far bigger waistlines than mine! I used to single out the main man and have a go back for a bit of fun. But your average barracker doesn't like that much and then it starts to get personal. They threaten to come over the barrier and it can easily turn nasty. I learned some time ago that you have to be careful, and these days I usually just respond with a smile and a wave and get on with the game.

The fans pay their money, so they're entitled to hand out a bit of stick. And to be honest, it's all water off a duck's back; I've learned to live with it. I just wish they'd come up with something a bit more original than pies and Japanese wrestlers. They've had long enough to think about it, after all. The trouble is, if you throw enough mud some of it sticks. And there really are people out there who seem to believe that I'm cricket's answer to Henry VIII (minus the six wives, of course).

When I was first picked for England's one-day squad for the Emirates Triangular Tournament with South Africa and Sri Lanka in 1998, most of the tabloid press churned out the usual rubbish about good old Oscar being the kind of guy who enjoys a few pints after a game and has a couple more in the pub on the way home, before collecting his fish and chips for supper.

One London-based paper rang up Colin Evans, who covers Lancashire for the *Manchester Evening News*, and asked if he could organise a picture that typified me. Colin knew what was coming. 'Er, like what?' he asked.

'Well, get him with a cricket ball in one hand and a big fat meat pie in the other. Know what I mean, my son?'

End of conversation. Colin never even bothered to ask if I was interested. How ridiculous can you get? Does anyone out there seriously believe that in this day and age, a professional athlete would last five minutes in his chosen sport if he lived that kind of life? Yes, I'm a big lad – 5ft 10in and around 15st. I've always had a healthy appetite. But I try to look after myself as well. Basically, I can't help the way I'm built: it's as simple as that. I've always been the same. If you thumb through my scrapbook collection, which goes right back to my early years with Haslingden in the Lancashire League, you'll see me described as chunky, burly, hefty, beefy, strapping, solidly built and so on. Like I say, it's the way I was made.

Some people are lucky and have no trouble with their weight. Take Graeme Fowler, my old Lancashire teammate. In his playing days, Foxy could drink like a fish and eat like a bloody horse, but never put on an ounce of weight. He was skin and bone. Not me, though. I did try to diet once, around ten years ago. I spent the whole winter on a slimming kick and lost two and a half stones. I didn't recognise myself when I looked in the mirror and I had to take a bit of flak when we reported back for the new season. We went off to Tasmania for our pre-season tour, and as soon as we got in the nets for some serious work, I felt as weak as a kitten. Alan Ormrod was our coach and, after keeping an eye on me for two or three days, he took me to one side and said: 'What's up, Oscar? You don't look right.'

I told him I felt completely washed out.

'You've been dieting, haven't you? How much have you lost?'

'Two and a half stones.'

'Right, well start eating again and put it back on.'

I did. And I've never tried to lose weight again. It has always been more of a problem for other people than it has for me. I am what I am. It's a bit late in the day for me to change. I'll go out and do my best and if people don't like it, so be it.

I'm not the only sportsman who's had this so-called problem, of course. I recall Colin Montgomerie, the golfer, trying to lose a few pounds and suffering exactly the same after-effects as me. Monty decided to revert to type and you couldn't exactly say he has struggled over the last few years because he's carrying a bit of extra weight. And what about Mike Gatting? He was supposed to be a few pounds overweight for most of his career but it didn't stop him leading his country, winning 79 caps and scoring over 4,000 Test runs. He didn't do badly at county level, either. What's more, despite his so-called lack of fitness, he played for Middlesex for more than 20 years. There are plenty more where they came from. Shane Warne has been named as one of the Five Cricketers of the millennium – and no one would claim he is wafer-thin. Nor were people like Ian Botham, Mark Taylor, Colin Cowdrey and Rod Marsh, yet they will be remembered among the true cricketing greats.

I'm certain I would have been chosen for England long before my first call-up in 1998 if I hadn't been saddled with the reputation of being the game's chief pie-and-peas man. If only people had looked at my fitness record since I joined the Lancashire staff in 1985, instead of listening to exaggerated tales about my eating habits. A detailed scrutiny of the record books would have revealed that I hadn't missed many games because of injury problems. In 1993, I picked up a thigh strain early on and tried to play through it though I should have rested for a week or so. As a result it got worse: I had to miss out for a few weeks, the team did well without me and I didn't really play any Championship cricket until late July. But I was still able to feature in all the one-day games.

I've also had a few niggles with my knees in the last two seasons – nothing serious, just the kind of wear and tear we all have to put up with. In the end, I had an operation during the winter before the 1999 World Cup. Apart from those two problems and a groin strain while I was playing in Australia in 1990–1991 and tried to remodel my action, I was injury free until I tore a calf muscle midway through the 2000 season. Not bad for a man whose main off-duty activity is supposed to be serious eating and drinking!

There is one game which should kick all those worries about my fitness into touch. It took place at Derby in the early '90s. We had all sorts of injury problems before and during the game. Graeme Fowler was skippering the side, and he came over to me at about 11.10 a.m.

'Do you think you can tie an end up for a little while, Bully?'

'How long have you got in mind?'

'Till lunch.'

'No problem.'

I plugged away right through the pre-lunch session, then put my feet up back in the tent and prepared myself for an afternoon at third man and mid-on.

That's when Foxy sidled over again. 'How do you feel about carrying on for a while longer?'

Here we go again, I thought. 'Any idea how long?'

'Till tea.'

So it was all hands to the pump again, right through the afternoon session and then a few minutes after tea for luck. I got through nearly 40 overs, on the bounce. Unfit?

It's no secret, of course, that I have my own views about the way we should train for cricket. I've never been a great believer in running, for example. These days the fashion is for players to put in hours and hours on the running track or pounding the streets. But it's boring. And it does absolutely nothing for your cricketing skills. Cricket is a stop-start game. Bowlers run in six times an over, then stop and have a breather.

Batters need to make short, sharp runs up and down the wicket. Fielders need explosive action between quiet periods. That's what our training should be geared towards, not to mention improving our cricket. There's always room for that.

Before the days when running took over, I used to play loads of squash and racquet ball, which is similar to squash except that players of a different standard can compete on more or less equal terms. I'd play for hours, building up my stamina, improving the hand-to-eye coordination which is a vital factor in cricket. It was competitive and fun. You could play until you were ready to drop, get a real sweat on and then finish with a shower and a laugh. Running? After 50 yards you start to wonder how much further there is to go. Mind-numbing. I'll go through with it, though, because it's part and parcel of the preparations these days. And down the years, I'd be willing to put my fitness record up against anyone else's.

Not that I don't like a bite to eat and a few beers or a glass of wine. And yes, I have been known to eat a meat pie. Is there anyone out there who hasn't? But chips with everything – no chance. The Austin household doesn't even possess a deep fryer. For breakfast, it's cereals and toast. When we're playing or training, I'll have a light lunch; whatever everybody else is eating. And in the evening, dinner is more likely to be chicken or fish than huge platefuls of Shepherd's Pie or Lancashire Hotpot. I try to keep red meat to a minimum. Veg? Steamed or boiled.

As it happens, I fancy myself as a bit of a cook. When I was little I always used to help my Mum get the Christmas dinner ready and it's gone on from there. I'm a fully paid-up member of Support Your Local Butcher, and even have one or two personalised brands of sausage. I take the seasoning round to my butchers, Brian and Andy Sanderson, and they make up the sausages. Delicious! And yes, that Ian Austin lookalike you've seen stocking up with fresh fish at Bury Market is the genuine article. I like to try different things. I don't go in for plain chicken or a piece of steamed fish. Instead, I'll do a spicy marinade or mix a sauce. I often do the evening meal – which means my wife Alex has to get on with the washing-up afterwards!

On the estate where we live in Baxenden, near Accrington, the neighbours joke that the first sign of summer isn't a cuckoo or a swallow – it's the smoke billowing out into the evening sky from Oscar's first barbecue of the year, washed down with a very sociable bottle of

Chardonnay! Just the job. I like good food, good wine and good company. I love my family: Alex and my two kids; Victoria, who is five, and Matthew, who is two. Not to mention Oscar, our Jack Russell – except when he's catching frogs in the back garden. I'm a true Claret, otherwise known as a fanatical follower of Burnley FC. And if there's a golf course nearby, I won't be far away. Handicap? Five.

I'm passionate about my cricket and proud of my record since I joined the Lancashire staff back in 1986. And if you'd told me then that I would still be playing first-class cricket in the new millennium, that I would have represented my country in the World Cup and played in eight Lord's finals for Lancashire, I would probably have agreed to put up with a few jibes about my weight.

Have a good read!

PART ONE

EARLY DAYS

I
IN THE BEGINNING

Saturday, June 8, 1985. Lancashire League. Haslingden 280 for two (I. D. Austin 149 not out, J. Entwistle 106 not out) Church and Oswald 177 for eight. An individual amateur record for Austin; a third wicket partnership of 268 between Austin and Entwistle, a league record for any wicket. The apprenticeship began around 15 years earlier.

When I was a kid my Dad, Jack, opened the batting for Haslingden and the whole family used to go along. My Mum, Ursula, helped with the teas while me and my three sisters, Carol, Susan and Janet, would be out playing with the other youngsters. There was always a game of cricket going on behind the pavilion, or else someone would have brought along a football and we'd have a kick around.

I wasn't yet dreaming of one day playing cricket for Lancashire and England, or even of playing centre-forward for Burnley (I was a Clarets fan even then). I just wanted to have fun. As I got a bit older, there was the added attraction of standing on the cattle market roof across the road from the ground and throwing back any balls that came flying over the perimeter wall. That was the prize job.

It never crossed my mind that one day I might follow in the footsteps of men like Clive Lloyd, Dennis Lillee, Andy Roberts, Geoff Lawson, Simon O'Donnell, Mike Whitney, Phil Simmons and Paul Reiffel, only a few of the international cricketers who, in the last 30 years or so, have strutted their stuff on the world stage . . . and played for Haslingden CC in the Lancashire League. Sometimes it's still hard to believe that the name of Ian David Austin is up there with those greats, in the Haslingden Hall of Fame. I never set out to be a star, you see.

Because of the family involvement, it was inevitable that I would play for the junior teams. I started in the Under-13s, where we played 20-over games against the other local Lancashire League clubs like Ramsbottom, Bacup and Rawtenstall and Greenmount of the Bolton League. We used to bat in pairs, with four overs for each couple and even then I invariably used to find myself as one of the last pair, either going out to win the match or trying to save it. I could bowl a bit, too. As the years went by, the kids in all the local teams gradually climbed the ladder, so by the time we reached the first team there were plenty of old friendships and rivalries around to make the competition that little bit tougher.

My mentor was Jack Dakin, who was involved with the club all his life. He must have spotted some potential in me because he took me under his wing and was always prepared to give me advice or extra coaching. One year, Jack took some of us along to a presentation night, where the team won a bat. I don't remember the ins and outs of it, but at the end of the season Jack presented me with this bat. It was a Stuart Surridge, autographed by David Lloyd. Even though it was far too big and heavy for me, it immediately became my dream bat. I spent all winter oiling it and tapping it in, and by the start of the next season it was perfect. The ball flew off it like a cannon. It was one of my most treasured possessions.

Jack kept pushing me and I spent a lot of time playing in older age groups, so even though I was quite a big lad for my age, it didn't do me much good because I always seemed to be up against older kids. I played at Haslingden High School, too, although it didn't help that I had a bust-up with the games master after missing a Lancashire Schools Cricket Association game – against Yorkshire, of all people.

The Association had played Essex at Old Trafford on the Saturday and were due to play in Yorkshire the following day. But I didn't have any transport and even though I left messages, they weren't picked up. When I arrived at school on the Monday, the games master called me in and gave me a fearful bollocking: I'd let down Lancashire, the school, the town, myself and anyone else he could think of. The headmaster gave a repeat performance immediately afterwards and I ended up being banned from the town team. They lost their next two games, after which

I was back in the bollocking room, getting the blame for the side losing because I hadn't played!

I also got into trouble for getting out after hitting 98 in 11 overs. The teacher pointed out that I might never get so close to a hundred again and I should have buckled down. Looking back, he probably had a point. But at the time I just shrugged my shoulders and walked away. I wasn't interested in hundreds; I had a bit of talent and I enjoyed hammering the ball around, but basically I just saw it as a bit of a laugh with my mates. One way or another, relations with the teaching staff were never quite the same.

There were no such problems at Haslingden. Around this time, people at the club were starting to sit up and take notice of Ian Austin, or Oscar, as I had become. Those of you with long memories will remember a television series called the *Six Million Dollar Man*. The hero was a guy called Steve Austin; his manager was Oscar Goldman. Carl Sudworth, a teammate of my Dad's and one of our junior coaches, combined the two and came up with Oscar Austin. And Oscar I have been ever since.

We were a great bunch of lads. We had grown up together, gone to school together and played football together, so playing cricket together was a natural progression. I must have had something, though, because when I was only 14, I started netting with the senior players four times a week and playing for the Under-18 side. In 1981, the Under-18s won everything in sight and I fully expected to be playing for them right through the following year.

One Tuesday evening early in the 1982 season, I strolled into the pavilion after net practice to find out where we would be playing the following weekend. The selection committee used to meet while we were practising and the lads would always look at the board for travel arrangements and so on. There was no I. Austin in the Under-18s. Instead, I was in the First XI to play Colne on the Saturday. I was also in the team for the Worsley Cup match against local rivals Ramsbottom the following day. I was just 15 years old. It took a while to sink in.

I don't remember being particularly nervous on the Saturday. We played 34 eight-ball overs in those days (as you can imagine, there weren't too many maidens) and I batted at seven or eight. We made around 180, and I finished up with 27 not out. I was pretty pleased with that, and so was our skipper when our opening bowler, Rod Taylor, got a wicket with the first ball. Apart from their professional, Collis King,

Colne weren't that good a side. I remember the senior players saying: 'With Collis coming in this early, we can let him get 70 or 80 and still win t'game.' He finished with 147 not out and Colne won with 13 overs to spare.

Collis's innings has always stuck in my mind. He was a fully-fledged Test all-rounder, who had appeared in a World Cup final and a string of one-day internationals for the West Indies. He took us apart. I couldn't believe anyone could hit the ball that hard, and always along the ground until he passed three figures. Then he knocked about six balls on to the cattle market roof and wandered off. Game over, thank you very much. Man against boys. Welcome to the Lancashire League, Oscar!

The cup game against Rammy was a huge one for us. They were our local rivals. Ramsbottom's pro was a Sri Lankan, Ashanta de Mel. We were in a bit of trouble when I went out to bat and he hit me with the first two deliveries; the first I ducked into and took a blow in the ribs, and I played the next one badly and got whacked again. I remember thinking: 'What the hell am I doing here?' But the third squirted off the edge to third man, and I was away.

Alan Massicks, who is still a good mate, was batting with me. At the start of the last over, I had 47 and Alan was around the same figure. He could easily have reached his own half-century, but instead he dead-batted the first ball of the over, took a single and then said: 'Right, now's your big chance, Oscar. Go and get a 50.' It was a tremendous gesture and it will stick with me for ever.

I said thanks by reaching my maiden half-century in Lancashire League cricket, and was rewarded with my first king-size hangover the next morning. The first of many, it has to be said. It has always been a tradition in the leagues that any player hitting 50 or taking five wickets is awarded a collection – his teammates take a cap around the ground and the punters show their appreciation, or otherwise, by the size of their donations. As it was a cup-tie and a local derby, there was £40 in the hat by the time the lads re-appeared, and that was a lot of money in those days. But Haslingden being Haslingden, it went behind the bar after the game and not into my pocket. My only memory of the night is waking up with a stonking great headache and not a penny left in the kitty, though I am assured a good night was had by all.

Still, easy come, easy go . . . and that is the way we played it. We all enjoyed a pint after the game and the classic line was: Win or lose, we'll go on the booze. Fortunately, as the years went by we drank more winning pints than losing, although back in 1982 we reached the final but lost to Todmorden. It was a controversial last-ball finish and as we left the field, no one knew who had won. The result was not finally decided until about half an hour after the game.

I stayed in the first team after that, gradually moving up the pecking order until I batted regularly at number four, and that's where I stayed. It was a tough school on and off the field. No one was going to do me any favours out in the middle, not least because the big name pros had a reputation to defend, which didn't involve being hit all over the field by a 15-year-old.

Even though I was the youngest in the dressing-room, I didn't escape the mickey-taking and the pranks. It was a case of sink or swim. If you couldn't hack it and were never going to get on with the others, there was only one option: go and play your cricket somewhere else. I suppose all dressing-rooms are the same. You're always going to get people acting the goat and you'll always end up on the wrong end of a few practical jokes. Down the years I've taken my share of stick, believe me. But you just bide your time and wait for an opportunity to get your own back.

There was a serious side to it all, though. By the time I was 17, I had left Haslingden High School with four O levels. Work wasn't easy to come by, and I started to wonder where I was heading.

Then Hartley Leroy Alleyne took over. Hartley was described in *The Cricketers' Who's Who* as a Barbados-born all-rounder, a hard-hitting right-hand batsman and a right-arm fast bowler. He toured Zimbabwe with the West Indies in 1981 and played for Worcestershire and Kent in the '80s. In answer to a question about how he spent the winter, he replied: 'On the beach, watching the sun set.' He described his cricketing habits and superstitions as 'joking with spectators'. In other words, he was quite a character. But to me, he will always be far more than that. Hartley Alleyne changed my life.

He joined Haslingden as our new professional in 1983, succeeding South African all-rounder Rob Bentley. He stayed with us until 1986, a spell which saw Haslingden win the Championship twice and finish in the runners-up slot once. And he altered my whole approach to cricket. He took me under his wing and tried to steer me in the right direction. He convinced me that it was worth working on my game. Until he arrived, I reckoned I was just a lad with a bit of talent who enjoyed his cricket and the company in the bar afterwards. But thanks to Hartley, it gradually began to dawn on me that I could make something out of the game. He pushed me onwards and upwards, put the idea into my head that if I used my talent properly I could play cricket around the world at someone else's expense.

In 1984, I responded to Hartley's encouragement by scoring six half-centuries for Haslingden, topping 400 runs in the season and taking more than 40 wickets. My form attracted the attention of the Lancashire Cricket Federation Under-19 selectors and I made my début against North Wales, taking six for 20-odd. In the next game at Derby, I hit an unbeaten 140.

Hartley arranged a trial with Worcestershire and their coach, Basil DiOliveira, was impressed enough to invite me back for a two-week stint. But I had to miss out on it, because I was involved with the Lancashire Federation in the annual Cambridge Festival. Dexter Fitton, who also went on to play for Lancashire and is still pro-ing in the leagues, was the captain and the team also included Nick Speak, now with Durham, and a young man by the name of Michael Atherton.

Athers was at Manchester Grammar School and came with a big reputation. But he was a couple of years younger than most of us, and was little more than a bag of skin and bones. He couldn't hit the ball off the square and the rest of us were swinging ourselves off our feet trying to keep the scoreboard moving along. But what a technique he had! And what determination!

I played one game for Lancashire Seconds, against Glamorgan at Lytham, scoring 30 not out and 15 not out and taking three for 20, good enough figures to earn me an invitation to the winter nets.

At the start of the 1985 season, I found myself out of work. So it was cricket, cricket, cricket. Hartley and I used to go down to the nets, just the two of us. He would spend half an hour trying to knock my head off and then I would return the compliment. We would adjourn to The Woolpack, the pub just across the road from the ground, for a couple of pints and a chat about cricket and then go back to the club in time for evening practice. My reward was an innings that rewrote the Lancashire League record books, earned me my first headlines in the national press and led all the way to a contract with Lancashire.

Yet the omens were not good as I joined John Entwistle at the crease in our game against Church on that Saturday in early June, 15 years ago. Ian Callen, Church's Australian pro, had dismissed both our openers with only 12 on the board. John and I were given a hard time, but we survived

– and how! We put on 268 for the third wicket, the biggest stand in the league's 110-year history. John finished with 106 not out and I hit an undefeated 149, which was at the time the highest individual score by an amateur since limited overs cricket was introduced in 1970.

Needless to say, I had never been interested in records. Until I had reached 137 with two balls of the innings left, I had no idea what the old record was, even though it was held by my Haslingden teammate Bryan Knowles. But the lads sent a message to me out in the middle, telling me that I needed two sixes off the last two balls to beat Bryan's 147. The Church wicketkeeper Tommy George got the message, too. He whispered: 'Look, Oscar, I'll stand back for these last two, then you can really give it a go!' The last two balls of the innings duly disappeared over the boundary and the name of Austin went into the record books.

The following Monday, the *Lancashire Evening News* reported that there were a few quiet drinks on the Saturday night to celebrate, but I can assure the reporter that the night was considerably more boisterous than that!

The next week there was a feature about me in the *Daily Express*, headlined: 'Presenting a likely lad to step into the shoes of Botham.'

I was on a roll. Three weeks later I hit my second ton, this time against Rishton. According to the *Sunday Express* reporter, it was 'as good an amateur's century as it has ever been my privilege to describe'. A week later, I was with the National Cricket Association Under-19 squad in an international tournament in Bermuda, and quite an experience that was too, both on and off the field.

There were times early on when things looked decidedly dodgy. The event is held every couple of years, with the venue decided on a rota system. We got lucky with Bermuda. And after two days' practice at Bisham Abbey, we flew out. There were two teams of us, NCA North and NCA South, to play against the likes of Ireland, Denmark, Holland and, of course, Bermuda, the host nation. There were three of my Lancashire teammates with me in the North side: Athers, Nick Speak and Warren Hegg. Yorkshire supplied a couple of players in Chris Pickles and Phil Berry and there were one or two others who went on to play first-class cricket. We landed, loaded up the bus and set off. Destination: Warwick.

Within seconds of our arrival, our dreams of luxury hotel accommodation were shattered. Warwick turned out to be a bloody great army camp. As we clambered off the bus, we were told which barracks to report to. Our home was just a big hut. Two rooms: one with a couple of showers and a couple of toilets; the other with 20 bunks. No wardrobes, cupboards, tables, chairs, nothing. After the usual chorus of 'I'm not 'aving t'bottom bunk if he's on top,' we had a bite to eat, a quick team meeting and settled down for the night.

It didn't last long. At about 4.30 a.m., one of the lads rolled out of his bunk and staggered off, half asleep, for a pee. He had barely got into his stride when the rest of the squad were woken by an almighty yell of: 'What the fucking hell is that?' We all leapt out of bed to see a lizard making its way across the barrack-room floor. This was no ordinary lizard. It must have been at least a foot long. By the time we'd decided it wasn't hostile and had seen it safely out of the hut, everybody was wide awake.

'What to do next?'

'Beach?'

'Beach it is.'

We all pulled on a pair of shorts and ran across the road to a beautiful beach straight out of the holiday brochures. Clear blue water, white sands, coral reef. Dawn breaking in a Caribbean paradise and all that. Gorgeous. Until yours truly decided to dive in off the coral and took a chunk out of the bottom of his foot. It was about two inches long and a clean scoop. I didn't really think anything of it at the time, but it was starting to throb a bit by the time we got back to the barracks. Sure enough, the physio's verdict was that I needed stitches.

'Hang on a minute, won't it be a bit awkward when I run in to bowl?' I asked.

'You'll not be doing any more bowling on this tour, Oscar. That's it as far as you're concerned.'

'Right. Never mind stitches. Just put a plaster over it and we'll take it from there.'

I hadn't come all that way to represent the North of England only to be told I would be on the next plane out. No chance. It was bloody sore, but it can't have affected my bowling too much as I finished up the leading wicket-taker in the competition.

By the time we got down to the proper business of playing cricket, things had taken a turn for the better off the field, too. Eventually the top of the hierarchy decided they had seen enough ants crawling across the floor and asked for better accommodation. The organisers agreed. So we were all shipped out to villas across the length and breadth of the island.

To make sure there was no North–South divide, every villa had two players from each of the English teams. I was with Speaky, Paul Atkins, who played a bit for Surrey afterwards, and Alistair Fraser, Angus Fraser's younger brother. It didn't take long to work out a rota system: first one up in the morning goes to the supermarket and stocks the fridge up with beer for after the game. As a bottle of beer in the bar nearby cost about three quid compared with three pence in the supermarket, it made a lot of sense. But even so, Alistair took a hell of a lot of persuading to part with his money. Must have been his Scottish blood.

The cricket went well. We reached the final, beating the South in a grudge match, but lost out to Bermuda in the end. By nine wickets. We managed around 160, with Athers hitting a 50 that went down like a lead balloon with the locals. There was just a polite ripple of applause. Our total never looked enough and their batsmen wasted no time in moving the score along. They batted well, but even so it was a bit of a surprise when the opener's 50 was greeted by a pitch invasion. Hundred of fans ran on and started stuffing things down his shirt and trousers. We couldn't work it out at all. The same thing happened when the number three reached 50 as well – and this time we spotted that the punters were stuffing banknotes down his gear. No wonder he looked happy. Between them they must have pocketed over a hundred quid. Athers spent the evening wandering around asking where he'd gone wrong.

At least he made it as far as 50, though. I struggled to get the ball off the square right through the tour. It was incredible, really. I had just broken the Lancashire League batting record and followed it up with another century against a top-line overseas pro. Yet on good tracks and near-perfect conditions in Bermuda, I could hardly score a run. In fact, I think the only time I reached the boundary was when the bowler took me by surprise by coming in off a couple of paces and letting go while I was still pottering around the crease. I was oblivious to the ball as it sailed towards me, hit the back of my bat and flew to the boundary. At least I had the decency to raise my bat in acknowledgement of the applause from the dressing-room.

I could live with poor batting form and a foot injury, though, and the only real downer of the trip for me was the day I bowled ten overs off the reel in near-tropical heat, trudged down to third man and nearly passed out. I was sure I was about to keel over. I had to be helped into the dressing-room, where I sat drinking pints of water with my head wrapped in a cold towel. An early lesson in the dangers of dehydration.

I finished the 1985 Lancashire League season with 496 runs, 26 wickets and a Championship medal. And to crown it all, on August 21, a letter dropped on to the mat. It was from Chris Hassall, the Lancashire secretary in those days. It was the offer of a two-year contract with Lancashire. It took me out of the dole queue and on to the first rung of the professional ladder.

I owed everything to Haslingden CC. The club had become a way of life for me. I had been steeped in Haslingden from childhood: I knew all about its history and traditions, and enjoyed listening to tales about the great players who had crossed the world to play for us. Men like Clive Lloyd. A legend! I was too young to really remember Clive when he played in the same side as my Dad in the late '60s, although I have a vague memory of a huge black man who always seemed to be hitting the ball out of the ground. But I bet no one watching Clive in action could ever have guessed that Jack Austin's little toddler would one day join him on the Lancashire staff. Perhaps that explains why Clive has always been one of my sporting heroes.

Another of the big name pros when I was a kid was Dennis Lillee, the great Australian fast bowler. Dad always recalls that Dennis was the first person to introduce a semblance of professionalism into Haslingden's amateur players, not allowing anyone on to the ground to practice until they had completed two laps of the outfield. Absolutely unheard of in those days! Dennis was at Haslingden in 1971, the year he made his Test début against Ray Illingworth's Ashes-winning side Down Under, and all the old timers remember him with huge affection.

Dennis always tries to call in at Haslingden when he is in the country and one year he arrived at the ground soon after the start of a game to be confronted by a belligerent young 13-year-old on the gate. 'Where's your money?' demanded the youngster as the fast-bowling legend attempted to drive past him into the car park.

'You don't seem to know who I am, son,' replied the great man. 'I'm Dennis Lillee.'

In true jobsworth fashion, the lad insisted: 'I don't care who you are, pal, you're not getting in here without paying.' Lillee duly paid up.

I can now reveal that the kid on the gate was a certain Ian Austin, and that Dennis Lillee has never allowed him to forget the incident. But I genuinely didn't recognise him – honest!

He's a good guy, Dennis, one of the breed of professionals who throw themselves into the job heart and soul, coaching the kids, taking net sessions, spending time in the evenings in the bar with members, sharing a drink with teammates and joining in all the dressing-room banter. And, of course, helping the club win matches.

West Indian fast bowler Andy Roberts, Haslingden's pro in 1981, came from a different mould. Andy was little more than a match pro. He would turn up at around 12.30 p.m., put his gear on, play his cricket and then get in the car and go home. While he was on the field he gave it everything, of course, and Haslingden were runners-up to Rawtenstall in his only season at the club. But like quite a few pros down the years, he found it hard to come to terms with playing alongside amateurs, people who did a job of work five days a week and were just playing their weekend cricket for fun. The dressing-room pranks were not for him, as he found out to his cost one evening at Bacup.

Bacup CC is perched on top of a hill and it can be a bit cold at the best of times. Two sweaters in the middle of summer, if you get the picture. The pavilion is on one side of the ground and the clubhouse on the other, so after the players have had a shower they have to hike across the ground for a pint. On this occasion Andy was last getting stripped off, and when he finally made it into the shower, some of the boys nicked his gear. When he reappeared, the rest of the lads had gone . . . and so had all his outdoor clothes.

After searching high and low in the dressing-room, Andy finally spotted his gear flying from the top of the flagpole by the pavilion. He was not best pleased. He ended up having to wrap a towel round his waist and haul down his clothes, with the rest of the players and a crowd of supporters from both sides cheering him on from the bar at the far side of the field. He was still moaning like hell about it weeks afterwards.

Great stories and great times. Without league cricket, I would not be where I am today. Haslingden and the Lancashire League taught me what the game is all about. OK, go out and give it your best shot every time. But a game of cricket never has been a matter of life and death, and it never will be. No team is ever going to win every week. The only thing that matters is being able to come off at the end knowing you have done your very best. You can't do more than that.

One day, when it is finally time to pack it in at Lancashire, I'll go back into the leagues. It's the least I can do. I'll play a bit of cricket, coach the kids, generally put something back into the game. And I'll have a hell of a lot of laughs as well.

2
LANCASHIRE CALLING

It didn't take Austin long to pick up the winning habit as a Lancashire player, helping the Second XI lift the Championship in his first season in 1986. It was a year that also saw his county début in a Sunday League game. But as Lancashire cricket welcomed a promising new recruit, some of the region's football clubs were left to dream of what might have been.

I didn't waste any time when the letter from Lancashire landed on the mat offering me a two-year contract. I knew the county had been keeping an eye on me and I'd had a word with Jack Bond, Lancashire's manager at the time, a couple of weeks before. I knew the score. So it wasn't as if the contract came completely out of the blue. Even so, I picked the phone up straight away, called Jack and asked for a meeting. I was going to give this a real go and I wasn't going to take the chance of playing a waiting game and then perhaps wondering what might have been in years to come. I went straight to Old Trafford, put pen to paper and that was that.

The local papers carried the story big time, with the old 'Dream comes true for Austin' line. But I knew damn well that at 19, there was still a long way to go. And even though I was on my way to Lancashire for the 1986 season, the winter of '85 still had to be taken care of. These days, Lancashire players are on year-round contracts, the only one of the 18 counties to offer full-time terms. But until the last couple of years, players were only under contract from April 1 to September 30, and in between times it was up to them to make a living.

As I said earlier, there wasn't a lot of work around – particularly for someone who would be packing the job in at the end of March to go off and play cricket for a living. Over the next few years, I had to find something to keep me off the dole in the winter, although it would have been a very different story if my football career had blossomed in the same way as my cricket. In fact, I might never have played for Lancashire at all if I'd stuck with football instead of packing it in when I was on the fringe of a professional career. Looking at the rewards available to footballers these days, I'll forgive you for thinking that Oscar lost the plot very early on.

I was a decent player as a kid, a centre-forward who ended up playing in central midfield because I was the best in the side. I played at school, played for the town team and one day when I was 15, Bolton Wanderers came along and asked me to go for trials. They ended up offering me schoolboy terms but it all ended in tears – for them, not for me. I was glad to be out of it. I just lost interest.

I used to play for my school on a Saturday morning, the town team in the afternoon, Bolton on a Sunday morning and then usually some kind of representative side on Sunday afternoons. During the week I had to train at night with the school, the local side and Bolton. What a bloody treadmill! Football was taking up every minute of my waking life. OK, I accept that most kids of 15 or 16 would jump at the chance to spend their lives playing football . . . but not me. In the end, it reached the stage where I'd simply had enough. Overkill. I took the boots off, chucked them away and said: 'That's it. Finished.' I didn't really play again for another four years, and then it was only for a bit of fun with the local pub team.

Bolton were disappointed, and when the news leaked out I had approaches from Manchester City, Bury and Blackburn Rovers. There were whispers that one or two other clubs might be interested. But I didn't want to know. I'd made my decision and I was prepared to stand or fall by it. And I have absolutely no regrets.

I still had to face the prospect of how to spend my time when I wasn't playing for Lancashire. It's a familiar tale for your average county pro. International players are away on tour and there are a handful of players who have a regular winter job to fall back on, often in things like public relations. But the majority have to get by as best they can. Down the years, there have been some strange jobs. Harry Pilling, the Lancashire batsman of the '60s and '70s, used to work for an undertaker! I solved the problem in the winters of 1987, '90 and '91 by playing in Australia and I'll be talking more about those trips later on.

In 1985, though, I was struggling to find regular work, so I was grateful for the chance to be involved with the Find A Fast Bowler scheme run by the former England and Lancashire paceman Peter Lever, who was the Lancashire coach. Every week, a bunch of hopefuls would turn up on a regular basis at the Indoor Cricket School in Withington, not far from Old Trafford, and spend the whole evening trying to knock the batsmen's heads off. None of them made the grade, except Peter Martin, my Lancashire teammate these days, who had already played for the Lancashire Federation and was there to help out. I was basically on the same tack. Some of the lads looked fairly useful indoors, but as soon as they got outside it was a different story.

From February 1, I was netting with the rest of the contracted players at Old Trafford. Two hours, two nights a week for two months; from six to eight. That was the extent of the winter build-up in those days. Eventually, 1 April arrived and I reported to Old Trafford for my first day as a Lancashire player. The first person I saw was Warren Hegg. Warren, or Chucky as he has always been known, and I go back a long way. We played in all the age groups together as well as lots of representative junior cricket. We had both been on the National Cricket Association tour of Bermuda the previous year, we joined the Lancashire staff on the same day and we've been pals and room-mates from day one.

And it was a good job Chucky was at Old Trafford on April Fool's Day, 1986, because nobody else was. The rest of the 30-odd contracted players were already up in the Lake District for a week of heavy duty pre-season training. Me and Warren, the new signings, the junior pros, were down to coach members' kids in the indoor school. We were absolutely gutted.

As it turned out, though, I was able to say to Chucky a week later: 'We've got a result here.' For while we were enjoying the quiet life coaching a few kids in the indoor nets, the rest of the boys were going through hell in the Lakes, running up and down mountains and all the rest of the physical stuff. When they got back they were shattered – although Jack Simmons was seen to be sporting a self-satisfied grin.

The story soon came out. On the final afternoon, the lads were dropped off in the middle of nowhere and told to round off their week by running back to the hotel. They set off with varying degrees of enthusiasm, and inevitably it wasn't too long before Simmo started to drop off the pace a bit. After about half an hour, the boys heard the growling engine of an old farm truck coming up behind them and sure enough, as it edged past, there was Jack sitting in the trailer at the back, complete with broad grin and regal wave. He didn't offer anyone a lift.

Simmo was one of the senior figures in the dressing-room and I suppose I might easily have been in awe of people like him, not to mention Clive Lloyd, who was still away with the West Indies, David Hughes, Graeme Fowler, Paul Allott, John Abrahams, Gehan Mendis and Patrick Patterson. Some of them were Test players and household names. But it was never a case of us and them – even though I ruffled a few feathers every now and then and earned myself a second nickname: Bully.

This came about partly because I was a big, strong lad, but there was another reason for it. As one of the junior pros, I had to do some of the more menial tasks around the place, like carrying the kit out to nets, or fetching the football if we decided to have a game after practice. You get the idea. On top of that, there was twelfth man duty for the first team: carrying the drinks, fetching sweaters on and off, doing a spot of substitute fielding. All the usual duties.

Well, on one occasion, I'd been running around like the proverbial blue-arsed fly, doing a bit of fielding here and there and running on and off with sweaters, drinks and everything but the kitchen sink. In the end, I was just about as knackered as the rest of the players when they came off after a long fielding stint.

'Put t'kettle on, Oscar, and make us a cup of tea.'

'Aye, that's it. And when you've done that, go and get us a few pies. We're starving.'

I wasn't having that. 'Put t'kettle on yourself,' I replied. 'I'm twelfth man, not a bloody gofer.'

There was a stunned silence for a moment or two. Then someone, I've a fair idea it was Simmo, said: 'Hey up, we've got t'playground bully in today!' The name has stuck, but there was never any bad blood after that little spat. Sure, Chucky and I were very much the new boys. But the senior players were fine with us and we'd both been into new dressing-rooms before. For the most part, we knew it was in our best interests to sit in a corner, keep our mouths shut and take it all in. And below that top layer of senior players there were people like Mike Watkinson, Neil Fairbrother, Ian Folley and Steve O'Shaughnessy, who were established county players but closer to our age group.

O'Shaughnessy always stood out. Watching him in the nets, I couldn't believe how much raw talent he had. He was just about the best batsman I'd ever seen – and he could bowl a bit, too. When he was in the mood, it was impossible to bowl to him. But somehow he was never able to take it out into the middle with him and after a spell at Worcester, he eventually drifted out of the first-class game. He still pros in the leagues, but at one stage it looked as if he was going to go all the way.

O'Shaughnessy was just one of many talented players who were around in my first season and with Speaky, Ian Davidson, Tony Murphy, David Makinson, Mark Chadwick, David Varey, Kevin Hayes and Soren Henriksen, among many others, also in contention, I soon worked out how hard it was going to be to get a game in the Second XI, never mind starting to push for a first-team place. Competition was huge. But I found myself in the seconds right at the start, and did well enough to stay there. I finished up playing 16 out of 18 three-day games, scoring 545 runs at 30.27 with a highest score of 93. I only bowled 89 overs, though, and ended up with eight wickets at 26.50 apiece. I played in most of the one-dayers, too. Above all, we went through the season unbeaten. Played 18, won nine, drew nine, lost none. And we won the Second XI Championship.

It was a season that introduced me to the delights, or otherwise, of life on the road, tearing up and down the motorways and living in hotel rooms. One of the most memorable matches on our way to the title was against Kent down at Folkestone, which meant we were able to celebrate an amazing victory on the team bus home without worrying about the breathalyser. It looked like being a close one at the start of the third day, when we batted on for an hour or so before setting Kent a target. Instead, we bowled them out for 24. I've never known anything like it. The wicket hadn't done anything out of the ordinary and was still playing OK, but Tony Murphy took a career-best six for nine, Soren Henriksen four for 12 and we rolled them over in less than an hour. We packed our bags, climbed aboard the bus and stopped 500 yards down the road at an off licence. By tradition, anyone notching a career-best buys the drinks, so Murph duly emerged from the shop with three cases of ale and the party started.

But there was nothing for Alan Ormrod, our coach, to celebrate when we took on Leicester at Grace Road. It was one of the two games I didn't play in, and will always go down as a good one to miss. I worked that one out as soon as I saw a Leicester teamsheet which featured George Ferris, Les Taylor and Jon Agnew, two England fast bowlers and a very sharp West Indian. Ormers was on the wrong end of a short ball from Ferris that smashed his cheekbone and made me feel eternally grateful to be doing the twelfth man duties. The crease was covered with Alan's blood and the game couldn't continue until the groundstaff had done a repair job with the sawdust.

Yes, Ferris was quick. But the fastest bowler we encountered that season was undoubtedly Devon Malcolm, who was just starting out with Derbyshire Seconds. Very rapid, our Devon! The wicketkeeper stood so far back you could just about jog a single as the ball went through to him. We met him in a one-dayer at one of the outgrounds. It was a big playing area and David Makinson kept picking Malcolm up off his legs and shovelling him over square leg. Devon's response was to bowl faster and faster, shorter and shorter, and he ended up going for a lot of runs, but he still had the last laugh on our opener, Mark Chadwick.

Mark had played against Devon before and was not too impressed with his fielding. So before the start of our innings, he said: 'Devon will be fielding down at fine leg, his eyesight isn't the best and while he's got a good arm, he hasn't a clue where the throw is going. Run the first one fast, push him for two and 99 times out of 100 you'll make it.'

We all nodded: 'Right, Mark.'

Third over of the day, Chadwick batting, Malcolm stationed on the fine leg boundary. Chadwick plays it down to fine leg, sets off like a bat out of hell and turns for the second just as Devon is picking the ball up. Result? Chadwick run out by ten yards. Devon propelled that throw like an Exocet missile, three inches over the stumps all the way. Chadwick never had a chance. Good decision, Mark!

Devon also took the opportunity to demonstrate his batting prowess in that game. We posted a decent total, and when they lost early wickets we were always favourites. But Devon came in late on and started swinging himself off his feet. He connected often enough to send the ball flying miles out of the ground on several occasions and have us seriously worried. But in the end, we pitched one up, knocked all three stumps out and that was it.

All in all, it was a great first season. And a lot of the credit for our success on and off the field has to go to the leadership of our captain, David Hughes, and to Alan Ormrod. David, or Yozzer as he is known to all comers, was 39 and had been a regular member of the Lancashire side for 20 years. It was widely assumed that in taking over as Second XI skipper he was easing out of the first-team picture. Instead, he did such a good job with us that the following year he was appointed county captain and went on to lead the side for another five seasons, winning three major trophies. Alan stepped up with him.

Yozzer is the best captain I have ever played for and I couldn't have taken my first steps as a professional under a better man. He was always completely straight. He led by example, and you couldn't fault his man management. Yozzer knew which players would benefit from a kick up the arse and which players needed a friendly arm around the shoulder at times. Like me, he would call a spade a spade if things needed sorting out in the dressing-room and then go into the bar for a pint and discuss the art of digging. Perhaps most importantly, he never held grudges.

A classic example of Yozzer's skill in handling his players occurred in a Sunday League game against Yorkshire at Scarborough in 1987, my first year as a first-team player. We went into the game with a bowling attack which featured Wasim Akram, Mike Watkinson, Andy Hayhurst, Jack Simmons – and me, the new boy. But despite my inexperience, I was called up to bowl my eight overs near the death. I remember thinking it was a bit steep to expect me to bowl at the end of the innings, but I bowled my first four and took something like two for ten. Not such a bad idea after all, then! At the end of my fourth over, Yozzer said: 'Right Oscar, have a break and then finish your spell at the other end. Waz wants this end.'

I lost it. I accused him of pissing me about, told him he might as well find someone else to bowl the last few overs and trudged off to the boundary. I was furious. Neil Fairbrother came running over. 'Have you refused to bowl?'

'No, I just told him I wasn't very happy.'

'OK. But whatever you do, don't refuse to bowl.'

'Right.'

I never had any intention of doing that, of course. So I switched ends, finished with three for not very many and then said to Yozzer as we were leaving the field: 'Can I have a word afterwards? I want to know what the bloody hell's going on.'

We won the game by two wickets and then the two of us hung around, waiting for the rest of the lads to go to the bar. Then Yozzer asked me if I wanted to step outside and sort things out. I still had steam coming out of my ears and let rip – I really let him have my twopenn'orth. Why was I asked to bowl at the death when there were far more experienced performers around? Why was I switched ends after doing so well for four overs? Yozzer's answer was simple and straight to the point. 'I agree with everything you say, Oscar. But the simple fact is that even though you're a junior player, I have more confidence in you in that situation than anyone else except Waz. I would put money on you to get it right. I'm sorry you've taken it the wrong way. But if you go away and think about it, perhaps you'll realise that this is probably the biggest compliment I could have paid you. Now, have you packed your bag? Right, let's go and have a beer.' For one of the few times in my career, I was speechless.

That certainly wasn't the case on another occasion early in my career, when I gave Yozzer another chance to use his diplomatic skills. Again, Yorkshire were involved, this time in a Second XI game at Crosby, one of the outgrounds, in 1986. We lost the toss and found ourselves fielding first. Richard Blakey was opening the batting for Yorkshire. Dick was then rated one of the game's top prospects and was in particularly good form at the time. He finished the season as the leading runmaker in the Second Championship, hitting 1,168 runs at 83.42. So when Yozzer threw me the helmet and box and told me to field at bat-pad, or Boot Hill as we sometimes call it, I should have known what to expect.

Murph opened the bowling and started off with a few looseners. I was immediately on the wrong end of a severe battering from Blakes. Shoulder, ribs, gut. The last ball was short and Dick pulled it with all his power. I got clattered again. That was it. I took off the helmet, threw it on to the ground and booted it across the pitch, shouting to no one in particular that the captain could find some other dick to stand under the helmet in future. Needless to say, all the players, including Blakey, were killing themselves laughing.

Yozzer was less amused. 'What the hell's going on?' he asked.

'I've finished under that helmet.'

'What do you mean? T'junior pro goes under the helmet and you're t'junior pro. So that's the end of it.'

'Well, this junior pro isn't going under that fucking thing any more. Here's the helmet, here's the box. I've had enough.'

David would have been well within his rights to read the riot act, and I could have ended up in deep water. But he recognised that getting peppered all day at Boot Hill just wasn't for me. 'Right, OK,' he said. And that was the end of the matter.

And it was the end of my days under the helmet, too – apart from the briefest of spells in a second-team game against Somerset. Mike Watkinson was having one of his rare outings in the Second XI and bowling his off-spinners. The batsman was Ricky Bartlett, another of the lads who had been in Bermuda in 1985. When I put the helmet on, Ricky started giving me all sorts of stick about what he was going to do to me. And sure enough, Winker eventually dropped one a bit short and Ricky really launched into a pull. I never moved. The ball caught me right on the badge of the helmet and I went arse over tit and landed on my backside. I was seeing stars for an hour. Goodbye, Boot Hill!

The Second XI Championship wasn't my only cause for celebration in the 1986 season, though. I also hit double top as Clitheroe's professional in the Ribblesdale League, helping them to lift the Championship and the Ramsbottom Cup. One or two clubs had been interested in signing me as pro the previous year, but I decided I would be better off having another season with Haslingden in the Lancashire League. I would have liked to stay with my hometown club in 1986 as well, but rightly or wrongly, Lancashire League rules prevented contracted county players from appearing in the league as amateurs. As I didn't know exactly how much Second XI cricket I would be playing in my first year – and with the kind of competition around at Lancashire, I was by no means guaranteed to be involved on a regular basis – I decided to try my hand as a league pro. Clitheroe came up with the best offer.

As it happened, they hadn't won the league since 1958 or the cup since 1965, so my speech at their annual Meet the Pro night caused quite a stir. To be honest, I wasn't expecting to be asked to speak, so when the chairman called for me to say a few words, I just mumbled the first thing that came into my head. 'It's great to be here and I want to enjoy every minute of it,' I said. 'I don't know much about Clitheroe's record over the last few seasons except that you haven't won much. But as you know, I've always played for a winning side at Haslingden and my aim this year is to put a couple of trophies in the cabinet here at Clitheroe.' Those words have gone into club folklore. It seems no one really gave us much of a chance pre-season, so doing the double was a tremendous performance. And even now, whenever I bump into anyone from Clitheroe, they always start the conversation by saying: 'Do you remember that Meet the Pro night back in '86 when you said . . .'

I had a good year, with 975 runs at 51 and 55 wickets at 14. But it wasn't all down to me, of course. Our overseas player, Grant Jordan from Melbourne, was a hell of a good cricketer, opening bat and gentle medium pacer. He did well, and Clitheroe was one of those sides where everybody chipped in at one time or another. We had a great team spirit, picked up the winning habit early and but for the ridiculous match rules, we would have wrapped up the title with about eight weeks left. Instead we had to go to the wire on the last day of the season.

I've always believed that in the leagues you should play overs cricket, with the side scoring the most runs taking the points. Simple as that. Instead, in the Ribblesdale League in 1986, the draw was thrown into the equation and sides could pick up a point for a so-called losing draw by batting second and not being bowled out. It encouraged players to defend, defend, defend.

The secret was to win the toss. You would stick the other side in, bowl defensively, keep them down to a low total and then knock off the runs. But if things didn't go according to the book and the opposition got a stack of runs, you could decide you had no chance of a win and just bat out time for a losing draw. Our problem was that we lost the toss just about every week and found ourselves being put in to bat. We would knock up 230 or 240, and then find the other side defending from the first ball for something like 120 for eight: three points instead of a maximum of six to the team who tried to win the game; one point to the side who just wanted to avoid defeat. It was a ridiculous system and no way to play cricket. I found it very frustrating and had my share of bust-ups with the opposition when they made no attempt to go for a win.

It all worked out for us in the end, though, and that spell at Clitheroe was an important part of a very steep learning curve for me that year. I was only 20, but as pro it was down to me to take on the responsibility and win the game for my team. There was no one else to turn to. I was the one who had to do the business when the chips were down. It was a tough year all round. I went into it thinking that playing cricket every day for a living would be a doddle. But after a full season with both Lancashire and Clitheroe, I was absolutely knackered. Not physically, but mentally. And I wouldn't recommend combining a first year on the county staff with a season as a league pro to a young player these days. It's too demanding – far better to get the feel of the county game first and then move in as a league pro in your second year. I got away with it. But it was bloody hard work.

Most importantly, 1986 was the year I made my Lancashire début in a

Sunday League game against Derbyshire at Buxton on August 10, 1986. It was completely unexpected. There was a telephone call from Jack Bond on the Friday night. 'Right, Oscar, you're in the 13 to travel to Buxton for the game on Sunday. Report to Old Trafford at 11.' I assumed I was just going along for the ride, number 13 out of 13, a chance to sample the first-team atmosphere. Instead, I was in the line-up.

Clive Lloyd was our skipper – and to think that all those years ago he'd opened the batting for Haslingden with my dad. I batted at eight and we were 149 for six when I went in. Michael Holding ensured I didn't hang around: caught Sharma, bowled Holding 4. But I did OK with the ball, with nought for 25 from my eight overs. Holding finished the game off with some huge hits and we were beaten by three wickets. A disappointing result and, looking back, I can't remember too much about the match – it's the same with a lot of people when they try to recall their county début. But I had been blooded.

3
BOTHAM B AUSTIN 3

New Road, Worcester. 2 May 1987. Benson & Hedges Trophy. Worcestershire 257-6 (G. A. Hick 88, I. D. Austin one for 41), Lancashire 170 (I. D. Austin 80). Austin's first victim as a county cricketer is a notable scalp indeed: England legend Ian Botham.

The 1987 campaign began with a trip to Jamaica, all expenses paid. Can't be bad! It was Lancashire's first overseas pre-season tour, and started a trend that has seen us travel to many countries, including Australia, Zimbabwe and South Africa as well as another trip to the Caribbean. I've been on them all and there are tales to tell of exploits on and off the field which I will return to later.

On that first Jamaican trip there were 18 Lancashire players, two coaches, a manager and a physio. Our hotel was in the centre of town, and on the first night we received our instructions from a bloke who arrived from the British High Commission: 'It's not the safest of areas round here and the locals aren't going to greet you with open arms. Never go out in groups of less than ten, never stray far from the hotel and above all, if one of those women across the road invites you for a chat, run a mile. She'll have someone lurking in the trees and if you're lucky he'll only have a knife.' In other words, welcome to paradise! So we spent most of our leisure time in the hotel, apart from a brief stay on the other side of the island in the tourist resort of Ochos Rios. That was a bit more like it.

And we played a bit of cricket. There was a game at Sabina Park against a Jamaican side captained by Michael Holding, the local hero. We also had our first meeting with Kenny McLeod, a distinctly quick youngster who eventually came and played for Lancashire. That was at a little ground somewhere in the middle of nowhere, just like village cricket back home. When we won the toss and decided to have a bat, there only seemed to be a few people in the ground, and very quiet, too.

We were going along quite nicely at first, getting in some decent practice and savouring the peaceful surroundings. But it all changed when Kenny came on to bowl. His third delivery was a bouncer which cleared Gehan Mendis's head by about a mile and was greeted by an enormous roar from the crowd. I don't know where they'd crept in from, but when Kenny unleashed that bumper it sounded as if there were about 4,000 in the ground. We were surrounded. It was Zulu Dawn all over again, and there was at least one bouncer an over from then on. Each one was greeted with the same almighty roar. But there was a tremendous atmosphere, great fun. When they batted, I was fielding down on the boundary edge and was laughing and joking non-stop with the fans: 'Come and have a puff of my cigarette, man! Have a drink of *real* Jamaica Rum, man!' I wasn't convinced about either option, but managed to keep everyone on my side. That was a great day and an early lesson in how to play along with the fans.

Meanwhile, back at Old Trafford, it was all change when the 1987 season finally got under way. Lancashire hadn't exactly been setting the cricketing world alight, so at the end of the previous season, Jack Bond and Peter Lever were relieved of their managerial and coaching duties and Clive Lloyd decided to call it a day as player and captain. They were replaced by Alan Ormrod as coach and David Hughes as captain, the two men who had been such a big influence on me in my first season on the staff in 1986. It didn't take me long to work out that their appointment was likely to be good news for me, and so it proved. In 1987, I forced my way into the one-day squad on a fairly regular basis and also made my Championship début. And I never stopped learning from Yozzer and Ormers.

I like to think that in 1986, they had both seen that I had the mental strength to go all the way into the first-class game. Cricket is played in the mind – it's all about attitude. Any kid who joins the county staff is a good player – he wouldn't be there if he wasn't. But raw talent isn't enough. How those players cope with difficult situations can be the difference between them missing out and making the grade. I'm not boasting when I say that I've always been able to handle myself in a tight corner. I have tried to work out what's needed and set my stall out accordingly. If it comes off, fine. If not, back to the drawing board. Either way, it all goes down to experience and into the bank for the next time around. David and Alan recognised those qualities.

Ormers was a tremendous coach. He had the ability to keep things simple and not baffle people with science. He could say more in five minutes than some coaches say in half an hour. He would always be ready to talk cricket. Ormers found time for you. And after something like 20 years on the circuit, there was hardly anything he didn't know about the players I was coming up against as I made my way in the first-class game: men like Norman Gifford, the former England left-arm spinner. Alan had played with Giff at Worcester for many years, so he knew all about his repertoire of tricks designed to unsettle the batsman. Giff had moved on to Warwickshire by the time I first encountered him. He had been playing first-class cricket for 27 years, while I was in my first season. But thanks to Ormers, I knew what to expect.

One of Giff's tricks was to abandon his full run and turn and come in off a couple of paces, hoping to catch the batsman off his guard. Coming, ready or not. Sure enough, soon after I arrived at the crease, Giff set off back towards his mark, stopped after two paces, turned and came in past the umpire, ready to bowl. I retreated towards square leg and Giff had to abort the delivery. He was not best pleased.

'What the hell do you think you're playing at?'

'I wasn't ready.'

'What do you mean, you weren't ready? A lad of your age has plenty of time to get ready in the time it takes an old so-and-so like me to get back to his mark.'

'I would have been ready if you'd bowled off your full run.'

Gifford went back to his mark muttering under his breath. He tried to pull the same move a couple more times but each time, thanks to Alan's advice, I was waiting for him and pulled away. In the end, he gave up.

Incidents like that were just small steps up the learning curve for me over the next couple of seasons, as I came to terms with the demands of the professional game. And early in the 1987 season came my sternest test so far: a Benson & Hedges Trophy group match against Worcestershire. And a gentleman by the name of Ian Terence Botham.

BULLY FOR YOU, OSCAR 45

It was our first game in the qualifying group, and it won't go down as the forerunner of Lancashire's great one-day exploits. We were beaten by 87 runs. But to make my début against Botham was fantastic. He had been my hero as a kid – he'd been every kid's hero, I suppose. We lost the toss and I had to wait a long time for my first glimpse of Both, thanks to Graeme Hick. Down the years, Hickie has made a habit of slapping the Lancashire bowlers around and this was to be no exception. He plundered 80-odd before he decided he'd had enough and it was time to let Both have a dart.

Botham's arrival coincided with my first over. He tucked one behind square early doors. But a couple of deliveries later, I got it just right and bowled him with one that nipped back enough to beat him. Botham bowled Austin 3. My first wicket for Lancashire. It doesn't get any better than that, does it? I kept it going OK from then on, and was reasonably happy with a return of one for 41 from 11 overs. But Worcester made an impressive 257 for six, and it would have been even more if the ball hadn't gone out of shape five or six overs from the end of the innings. Did I say out of shape? The thing just about exploded. Normally when a ball breaks up it splits down the seam, but this one came apart right across one side. No wonder the later batsmen were struggling to get it off the square!

As we came off at the end of their innings, I noticed Yozzer heading straight for the umpires' room. I didn't think anything of it at the time. But in a couple of minutes he reappeared in our dressing-room, tossed me the battered ball and said: 'There you are, Oscar. The ball that got you your first wicket for Lancashire. Look after it.' I did. I still have it to this day. The ball that bowled Botham. I wonder if Beefy still has the ball that did for me a couple of hours later. I doubt it, somehow.

We had collapsed in a heap at 80 for six when I picked up the bat and walked out of the dressing-room. Instead of the usual polite applause, all I got was: 'Oscar, you've forgotten your helmet!' from the rest of the lads. I turned round. 'I haven't got a bloody helmet,' I said. Looking back, it might have been an idea to invest in a lid before going out to face an attack featuring Both, Graham Dilley, Neil Radford and Phil Newport. But until then, the thought had never crossed my mind. I soon put matters right, though.

Against bowlers of that calibre on an early season New Road wicket, I quickly found myself playing and missing and scratching around while wickets tumbled at the other end. And it wasn't long before John

Stanworth joined me at 119 for nine. I assumed Stanny would want to play a few shots and get it over with, but instead, he came in and started blocking as if his life depended on it. With me struggling to get a bat on it at the other end, it must have been pretty dire stuff.

The Worcester players certainly thought so, because it wasn't long before the slip cordon started to get restless. Steve Rhodes, the Worcester keeper, has never been short of a word or two and he was chirping away at us. Both, too, was clearly getting fed up with the whole business. His red wine must have been coming up to room temperature. Eventually, Beefy decided enough was enough: 'Come on lads, we're getting bored here.'

I was straight back at him. 'Right, come on then. If you want a proper challenge, get down the other end and have a bowl yourself. You're a bloody old man; well past it. Let's see what you can do.'

It was like a red rag to a bull. Both wasn't going to take that from some young unknown. He grabbed the ball and came charging in. Just the job! That was all I needed to play a few shots and this time I was connecting. Judging by his response, Beefy was not impressed. I sailed past 50 and was starting to think in terms of a ton when I tried one heave too many, and out went the middle pole. Austin bowled Botham 80. Both's reaction was to run down the wicket, put his arm round me, shake my hand and say: 'Well played, lad – come and have a beer.'

As it happens, I had two. And the whole incident tells you everything about Both. He had never set eyes on me before, and I had just hit him all over the field. I can think of a lot of players who would have sent me on my way to the pavilion with a few well-chosen words. But Ian wasn't that kind of bloke. On the field, he was as hard as iron and he'd do whatever he could to win. But once the game was over, it was time for a drink and a chat. That's how I was brought up to play the game at Haslingden, and that's how I've played it ever since. Simple, isn't it? And if a cricket legend like Ian Botham can do it, why the hell can't everyone else?

We were back at New Road the following day, this time in the Sunday League, and once again I collected a notable scalp for my first wicket in the competition. Hick bowled Austin 3. Not bad going – first victim Botham, second victim Hick. The down side was that we lost both matches.

I had to wait until June for my Championship début against Derbyshire at Derby. It would have taken even longer but for a Roses

Match bust-up the previous week that ended with Jack Simmons collecting a two-match ban. Yorkshire's last pair, Dick Blakey and Stuart Fletcher, held out for nearly 18 overs for a draw but everyone west of the Pennines was certain that Fletch should have been given out caught at bat-pad not long after he came in. Simmo had a few choice words to say about it afterwards, which were spread all over the national press the next day – yes, county cricket actually received some publicity back in 1987. He accused Fletch, who went on to play for Lancashire for a couple of seasons a few years down the line, of cheating. The Lancashire committee weren't happy about it and Jack was suspended. Enter Oscar.

I must admit, the butterflies were fluttering a bit as we warmed up before the start of play and even though I was down to bat at seven, the early overs suggested I wasn't going to be sitting on my backside in the tent all day. As ever, Derby had a more than useful seam attack, featuring Michael Holding, Ole Mortensen, Allan Warner, Paul Newman and Martin Jean-Jacques, and they made early inroads. We were 135 for five when I joined Mike Watkinson. I reached the middle, took guard, patted the wicket a few times – anything to put off that first delivery from Holding, who was standing somewhere in the middle distance looking a million times more menacing than he had in our pre-season friendly at Sabina Park.

The first ball was full length. It hit me on the foot and cleared off towards fine leg. I reckoned it was a safe single. But Winker had other ideas. So, ball number two – another full-length delivery, and this time I got a bit of bat on it. I'd have settled for one to fine leg, but this time Winker was going flat out and I ended up scampering two at top speed. After that, I got stuck in fairly well and survived everything Michael could throw at me before Mortensen, the Mad Dane, trapped me leg before for 37. I put on 59 with Winker and then 53 with Ian Folley for the eighth wicket, earning myself a few headlines the next day. There was 'Allegro Start By Austin' in one paper, 'Austin Safety Drive' and then 'Durable Austin Steadies Lancs' in one of the broadsheets. How did you guess I'd kept my scrapbook from day one?

The match looked set for a decent finish when we led by 178 at the end of the second day of three. Then we arrived the next morning to find the outfield under about a foot of water, and that was that.

I played in the next game against Kent at Liverpool, taking my first Championship wicket when I clean bowled Neil Taylor for 49. I also dismissed Alan Igglesden and Derek Underwood to finish with three for

28 from 19 overs in their first innings. Then Simmo returned from his suspension, and I was back in the Second XI for the rest of the season, with a few Sunday League games thrown in. That didn't worry me – I'd made my mark. People knew I was around.

I was also able to make a brief return to the Lancashire League as Accrington's pro when Bertie Arun, an Indian all-rounder who was their original choice, was injured.

The year 1987 was a memorable one. Why? In short, Viv Richards. Viv's signing for Rishton during the winter caused a sensation, for the days when the world's leading players would arrive in east Lancashire every summer to play as professionals had long gone. I don't think people really believed Viv would actually play in the league until the day he flew in by helicopter for his first game. It made the national news on television and radio.

Viv did an incredible job on and off the field. In a wet summer, he topped the batting averages with 899 runs at 64.21, and also took 42 wickets. He was like the Pied Piper; everywhere he went, there was a near full house. Club treasurers were delighted. And he never let the fans down. After the game, Viv would spend hours signing autographs – and I do mean hours. He would stroll into the bar, buy a couple of drinks and then sit in a corner, signing away until he finally reached the end of the queue. Viv was great with both his teammates and his opponents, too. Everyone was in awe of him, of course, but he did his best to be one of the lads. On top of that, he also put in plenty of time coaching the kids. That's how a pro should behave!

I only played eight games compared with his 17, but finished second in the averages with 428 runs at 61.14. Steve Waugh was third in the table on 56.73, so I was in some pretty good company. Waugh was just a young lad at the time, spending a season with Nelson as he started to make a name for himself with New South Wales in the Sheffield Shield. I only encountered him once and I was on the receiving end of six bouncers in a row, accompanied by a few Aussie expletives after each delivery. But he soon found out he was wasting his time.

Overall, 1987 was a big year for me. I had joined the staff 12 months earlier as a batter who could bowl a bit. But during the 1987 season, I worked and worked on my bowling. And thanks to some friendly wickets on the outgrounds, I produced a few pretty useful performances in Second XI Championship games, too – like match figures of 12 for 67 against Warwickshire and six for 33 from 20 overs against Somerset.

I maintained that kind of progress over the next couple of seasons, until I was a regular member of the one-day side. I was squeezing in a few Championship games as well, either when regular players were on England duty or we had a few injuries. I reckoned I was worth a place on a more permanent basis, of course, and it got a bit frustrating when I was in and out of the side. I felt I was in danger of being branded a one-day performer who couldn't hack it in the longer game. I knew I could – if only I was given a real chance. There were a few whispers from elsewhere. Nothing concrete. Just people who I didn't really know stopping by for a chat and letting the conversation turn to when my contract was due to run out.

But even though I wanted to play regular Championship cricket, there was no guarantee I would get it anywhere else. And I was a Lancashire lad, after all. I'd grown up in Lancashire and it had never really crossed my mind to play for another county. With six Championship games out of a possible 22 in '88 and another eight in '89, I was at least part of the set-up. And we struck gold by winning the Sunday League play-off in 1988 and the league itself the following year.

My county cap came completely out of the blue. I'd started 1990 determined to take that last final stride and become a regular member of the Championship team. That would have been more than enough for me. But instead, it was just the start. I was on the winning side in two Lord's finals, we finished second in the Sunday League and sixth in the Championship. Above all, I was capped.

There was nothing at all in the wind as I nursed a king-size hangover all the way from St John's Wood to Old Trafford on the day after the Benson & Hedges final. We'd beaten Worcester by 69 runs, and it was quite a party afterwards. We were all either half asleep or feeling desperately sorry for ourselves as we climbed aboard the team bus the next morning and headed north for a Sunday game against, would you believe it, Worcester. Yes, Botham and co. played a big part in my early career.

The game was due to start at 2 p.m. and the bus didn't reach Old Trafford until about quarter past one. So there was a bit of a panic when we got a message that all the players had to report to the committee-room. Congratulations for winning at Lord's? A bollocking for being late? An inquest into our celebrations the night before? Nobody quite knew.

I filed in somewhere in the middle of the line, and was vaguely aware of the chairman, Bob Bennett starting to say a few words: 'It gives me great pleasure to be able to award a county cap to Ian Austin.' I didn't hear any more. It was all a blur as I stumbled across the room, shook hands with the committee men, collected my cap and trooped back to the dressing-room with the rest of the boys. Everybody shook my hand or hugged me and said: 'Well done, Oscar!' Then it was out on to the pitch for a formal announcement to the fans and members, and another presentation in front of the pavilion, this time from Yozzer. Pictures for the press, a few words here and there. I felt a million dollars. It was the perfect hangover cure – and a ready-made excuse to start celebrating all over again as soon as we had seen off Worcester!

4
ON TOP DOWN UNDER

One of Austin's proudest possessions is a scrapbook. Entitled *The History of Ian 'Oscar' Austin*, it was presented to him by Maroochydore CC, Queensland, after his second spell as the club's overseas player in 1992. The Aussies, both at Maroochydore and at the Randwick club in Sydney, loved Oscar. The feeling was mutual.

I've mentioned earlier that finding winter work was never easy in my first few years on the Lancashire staff. In those days, when the season ended it was a choice of finding something to keep the finances ticking over or the dole queue – and I've been there in my time, too.

I've done a bit of work in local shoe factories and some labouring. I once worked for a mate who was a cabinet maker and did a winter and a half delivering beds for a local firm. It was a question of finding something to make ends meet, instead of signing on the dotted line every couple of weeks. But your guess is as good as mine as to where the story that I spent my winters as a gravedigger came from. That is pure fiction.

The best job of the lot was in 1988, when I worked for Slinger's Butchers in Great Harwood, not a million miles from Haslingden. I was in the unloading bay. There were four of us: Dickie, the foreman, Andy, Ferret and me. Our job was to unload the carcasses when they arrived on lorries from the abattoir and hump them into the boning-room. Heavy work, and it didn't half strengthen me up. Dickie was about 6ft

4in and as strong as a bloody horse. He expected everybody to lift carcasses around like he could.

We arrived at 7 a.m., and the first there clocked all four of us on. There would be two or three vans waiting to be unloaded, so it was on with the white cap, overalls and wellies and straight into action. The deal was that as soon as the vans were empty, we could go home. That was perfect for me. I was happy to work like hell if it meant being able to pack in at lunchtime and go and have a round of golf. And that was no problem for Dickie. He wanted the job done, too, and kept us hard at it.

But it wasn't all work and no play. It didn't take Dickie long to figure out that as a pro cricketer I'd have a good arm and would be a useful man to have around for the fat fights. We'd strip lumps of fat off the inside of a carcass and hurl them at one another. You learned fast how to catch or get out of the way, I can tell you. If you got hit, it hurt! Another of Dickie's specialities was to put a big blood clot down one of your wellies. I leave the rest to your imagination. Great fun, though. And nobody batted an eyelid at the sight of a Lancashire cricketer unloading carcasses of meat for a living. I was just one of the boys. And that's how I've always wanted it.

A year later, I was coming to the end of the season and wondering what the winter might have in store for me this time when David Makinson asked me if I fancied playing in Australia. He had been with the Maroochydore club in Queensland for the last couple of years, but couldn't make it this time. How about it, Oscar? He didn't need to ask twice. A young lad learning the game, a chance to go to Australia and see the world, all expenses paid, accommodation provided. Why not? What better way could there be to spend the winter than basking on the Sunshine Coast of Queensland? So I left as soon as our season ended and had a week to acclimatise before the Australian season got under way – not like my next two trips when I got off the plane, into my whites and on to the field.

That first time, I arrived in Maroochydore on the Saturday afternoon after 24 hours on a plane, half knackered. I was staying with Ron and Pat McMullin, just round the corner from the ground. It turned out to be a home from home for the next six months or so. Should I go down and meet the players? Or should I turn in and have a kip? I met the players. They were painting the pavilion, paint brushes in one hand, bottles of beer in the other. It quickly turned into a Meet the Pro afternoon. At about five o'clock one of the lads went out for a couple of buckets of Kentucky, the beer flowed and we all ended up absolutely plastered. Welcome to Oz!

It was the perfect way to start. They were a great set of lads; so laid-back. They accepted me from the word go, and just wanted to play some good hard cricket and have a hell of a lot of fun afterwards. I'm always happy to go along with that kind of scenario. We played in the Heritage Shield First Division, a district competition. Two-day, two-innings cricket on successive Saturdays. There was also a tournament between representative sides from each area. We were the Sunshine Coast and I played for them, too.

Maroochydore were known as the Black Swans. The first game was against Tewantin-Noosa, one of the stronger sides. They had a quickie called Kent Officer, who was reckoned to be a bit useful. I got the standard greeting: the first three balls around my earhole followed by 'Welcome to Australia, you Pommie Bastard!' This Officer wasn't exactly a gentleman. I didn't get so many in the first innings, but we bowled them out cheaply and when I went in again the following week, Officer was waiting. The verbals started again and for 20 minutes or so, he kept banging everything in halfway down and handing out the abuse. Eventually it got to the point where I'd had enough. So I waited for the right delivery, ran down the wicket and hit him straight back over his head for six. He never said another word.

I was always ready to give the Aussies as good as I got. Always will be. But it didn't stop me getting on really well with them all.

The representative games were played on the Sunday, but that year the Sunshine Coast were a poor team. There was far too much of the old pals' act when the side was chosen and we never really played our best 11. But even though we didn't fulfil our potential at club or representative level, it was a wonderful time on and off the field. As I say, it was like a home from home with Ron and Pat. Ron was club president and looked after the ground as well. He lived and breathed cricket, and Pat used to moan like hell at the amount of time we spent at the club. She had a point. I spent hours and hours down there. Two evenings a week I coached the juniors, and there were two more nights with the senior players. I helped Ron with the square and after practice I usually stayed around for a couple of beers. It was always 'Your tea's in the microwave' when we finally got home. Then after a meal, out on to the balcony again for more cricket talk.

Sometimes I would be in bed by ten and up again at six. It was that kind of life. And that's where I started playing golf seriously. Maroochydore fixed me up with a membership and a set of clubs and there was always someone looking for a game, either from the cricket club or one of the members.

It really was a wonderful time. Everyone involved with Maroochydore went out of their way to make me feel at home. Great people. A few of them have been over to visit us and I've stayed in touch with a lot more, either by letter or abusive phone call.

Two years later I had another opportunity to play in Australia, this time thanks to Mike Whitney, the Test fast bowler who was Haslingden's professional in 1990 – a good pro and a top man. We had a beer together every now and then while he was at Haslingden, and he offered to fix me up for the winter. He played for the Randwick club in Sydney First Grade cricket, which was a high standard. When the New South Wales boys weren't involved in Sheffield Shield matches they played for their clubs, so at any given time you might run into Australian Test players. Like I say, a good standard.

One weekend we played against Bankstown. We batted on a real green top and reached around 180. But we soon made inroads, and at the end of the day had five down, including a wicket with the last ball. A week later, we returned to finish the game. We followed the umpires out into the field, then along came the batters. The new man was a guy called Steve Small, who just happened to open the innings for New South Wales and finished up leading runmaker in the Sheffield Shield that season. I couldn't work this out at all. He hadn't even been in the side a week earlier, and here he was coming in at number seven. I asked Whit what was going on and was told that it was OK to make changes between the weeks, providing you were swopping like for like. But you couldn't replace an opening batsman with a Test fast bowler, for instance.

'Right. So how come the New South Wales opener can be brought in to bat at seven?' A fair question, I thought.

'Well, he's captain. They've left the skipper out and Steve has taken his place.'

'Oh, I see.' But I didn't really.

My first ball was a good 'un: Small edged to first slip. Dropped. Third ball, edge to second slip. Dropped. He went on to get 90. Whit was bowling at the other end and soon got rid of the overnight batsman. Who came in at number eight? Steve Waugh, a man with a couple of Test hundreds to his name already.

'What the bloody hell's happening, Whit?'

'Well, Steve's an all-rounder with the Shield side, so they've left out the all-rounder who played last week and brought him in.'

Number ten was Wayne Holdsworth. At least he was a genuine tailender, but he was also just about the fastest bowler around, and was a class above anyone we'd encountered the previous weekend. He spent the next few hours trying to cave my head in. In the end, it was obvious that no one was going to win so we called it quits and headed off to the bar.

Overall, though, I did well, after a chaotic start. Typical Whit. He fixed up the flights and everything, and Alex and I decided to have a three-day stopover in Hong Kong. We were due to arrive in Sydney on a Saturday morning and the plan was for me to have a nice easy week before the first match. Unfortunately, Whit got his wires crossed. His Dad picked us up. 'We'll drop your bags off where you're staying, but leave your kit in the car because we're going straight to the ground. We couldn't risk you in the first team in case the plane was delayed, so you're playing Third Grade. They don't start until one o'clock, instead of ten for the first team.'

Fortunately we were having a bat, but we'd already lost two wickets by the time I arrived at half past one. 'Right, get your pads on, you're in next.' Ten minutes later, I was walking out to bat, still rubbing the sleep from my eyes and trying to work out roughly where I was. I played and missed for about half an hour, but the bowling wasn't of a great standard and once I started middling it, I was away. I ended up with 130.

After catching up on my sleep and a bit of a bat and bowl in the nets, I made my début for the first team the following week. I took five wickets for not very many and I was up and running. I had a good season. I finished up on top of the batting and bowling averages with 465 runs at 33.21 and 34 wickets at 16.97.

The Randwick track wasn't the best in the world by a long way, mainly because it was sand-based, being right down by the beach. The groundsman – sorry, curator – had to give it a good watering on the morning of the game, so I made sure I got my hands on the ball early doors and I kept it until lunch, by which time the pitch had dried out. Then it was a case of 'There you go lads, job done'. And I'd hand over to the spinners.

Sydney was a marvellous place to live. The club found us a house in a suburb called Coogee, overlooking the beach, and that's where we spent most of our time. Alex had a job behind the bar in the Randwick rugby club so, not surprisingly, we put some time in there, too. We did all the sights, made some great friends and left for home with a load of great memories.

We stayed in England the following winter, but Maroochydore wouldn't take no for an answer at the end of the 1991 season, so we set off again. They fixed Alex up with a job to keep the finances ticking over and I was made club captain as well as captain of the Sunshine Coast side. I didn't do a bad job, either. The Black Swans topped the league table and reached the Grand Final and Sunshine Coast lifted the Wide Bay Super Series, the regional competition. That was a massive achievement. They had never reached the final before.

At my first meeting with the selectors, I set my stall out. I told them I would only skipper the side if I could have a say in who played: 'If we're going to compete, we need our best players. If someone isn't good enough, he doesn't get picked – never mind who his mates are. If not, count me out.' They agreed.

We were very competitive. We only lost once. And our victory in the final was one for the Red Rose Hall of Fame, with a vote of thanks to a certain Pakistani all-rounder. I made 104 not out in our total of 218 for four off 50 overs but our opponents, Maryborough, looked to be cruising early on. That's when I decided to bring on 'Wasim Akram'. I hadn't spent many hours alongside our Wasim Akram out in the middle or in the nets without picking up a tip or two about seam bowling. So with the game just starting to slip away from us, it was clearly time to give our own left-arm quickie, Paul Seamer, a bit of Lancashire wisdom.

I was fielding at mid-on so I ambled over, handed him the ball with the seam apparently set for an away swinger and said: 'Right, put your fingers here, run in and bowl the bloody thing as fast as you can a foot outside off stick.'

He looked at me as if I was mad. 'I'll miss the strip by a yard if I let it go like that.'

'Never mind that. I'm captain, I'll take responsibility if it goes pear-shaped. Just run in and let it go. And fast!'

He did. The batter saw what was coming, shouldered arms and his middle pole flew out of the ground. Instead of celebrating, Seamer stood in the middle of the wicket looking stunned. 'What the fuck is happening?'

'Just keep calm and do what I tell you. This time, hold the ball like this and start it a foot outside the leg stump. Fast as you can.'

He obviously thought I'd gone completely mad this time, but the lad was a good 'un. He did as he was told, the ball swung in a mile and bingo, out went the leg stump. Seamer finished with three for 48, I chimed in with two for 28, the last five or six wickets went down for nothing and we won by 15 runs.

Back in the dressing-room, Seamer and the rest of the boys couldn't wait to find out how I'd done it. 'Oh, you'll learn in good time,' I told them. 'But I've never given you Aussies any tricks of the trade, and I'm not going to start now. And while you're at it, get that bloody champagne open!'

As a consolation, I fixed Paul up at our local club, Baxenden, in the Ribblesdale League the following year, but he hardly took a wicket.

At club level, we led the way from the start – once I had got my act together after flying in from Singapore just two hours before leading the boys out against Yandina. But I managed to chip in with three for 21 off 15 and we bowled them out for 76. It was the start of a roll that saw us finish on top of the pile. Unfortunately, that only meant a passport into the play-offs, and even before a ball was bowled we knew we would be without three key men, including me. I was due to report back to Lancashire in mid-March, so I had to fly out and leave the boys to it. They were beaten in the final. It was an anti-climax but on a personal note I had come within a whisker of finishing with 1,000 runs and 50 wickets and I was described in one write-up as 'the Sunshine Coast's finest-ever import'.

It had been another great six months and those three spells Down Under represented a tremendous learning curve for me. For starters, I had to come to terms with two-innings, two-day cricket played over two weekends. It certainly concentrated the mind as far as batting was concerned. The problem was, if you missed out on the first weekend you could find yourself waiting for the best part of a month before getting another chance, depending on the weather and how the game went.

It was good cricket, though. Batters had longer to build an innings and the fielding sides knew they would have to take wickets and bowl the opposition out. Could it work here? I doubt it. The weather would work against it, for one thing. Given a fair crack of the whip, conditions are usually the same week in and week out in Australia. But not here. You could go out one Saturday, find perfect batting conditions and pile up 250 or more in the first innings. Seven days later, it might have chucked it down all week and you'd be in a bowlers' paradise. The side batting second wouldn't have a chance.

But I've only happy memories of my time in Oz. The people and the lifestyle were marvellous and I've always fancied going again. But first the kids came along and we wanted them to be born in England, then at the end of the 1998 season, when there was talk of another trip, I found myself touring with England ahead of the World Cup. Ideally, we would have liked to take Victoria and Matthew out there for a season before school started – but now we've run out of time.

It's a hell of a good life, though, and I would recommend it to any young player who gets the opportunity. I don't entirely rule out living over there when I finally pack it in: it would be a big decision, but we have talked about it.

PART TWO

GOLDEN DAYS

5
MY SUNDAY BEST

Sunday, 21 July 1991. Lord's. Lancashire, chasing 144, are reduced to four runs for four wickets. They recover to 39 for seven before going on to defeat Middlesex by one wicket. Their success is built on an eighth wicket stand of 105 in 23 overs by Austin and Warren Hegg, a competition record.

I walked out to join Warren with Lancashire on 35 for seven. Fowler, Atherton, Lloyd, Fairbrother, Watkinson, Wasim and DeFreitas were all back in the tent and we still needed another 108 to win.

'What do you reckon, Oscar?'

'I reckon we're in the shit.'

'What are we going to do about it?'

I just laughed. So did Warren. I mean, what could we do?

'Let's just enjoy ourselves,' I said. 'We've nowt to lose. If we get beat, it's not our fault. There won't be many fingers pointed in our direction. If it's anywhere near, belt it. If not, either let it go or keep it out. You never know what might happen.'

The good news was that Norman Cowans had bowled his eight overs right through and had finished his spell. The bad news? He'd taken six for nine.

More good news. They were a bowler short and would have to find someone to fiddle the missing eight overs. Mike Gatting ended up bowling five-and-a-bit overs, and Paul Weekes two.

So we slapped a few fours here, poked a few singles there. Kept out the straight ones. Before long, we'd added 50. At the end of each over we'd have a chat. The message was always the same. 'Keep it simple, we're not going to win but we're not going to give it away either. And let's enjoy it while it lasts.' Then the stand was worth 75. 'Hey up, we can do this.' All of a sudden, things had started to get a bit serious.

With two overs left, we passed the 100 partnership and at the start of the final over, bowled by Gatt, we needed just three to win. I didn't help the cause when I was run out off the first ball, but the momentum was with us and David Hughes saw us home with one delivery to spare.

Looking back, I sometimes wonder: how the hell did we do that? But we were young, we had nothing to lose and we just went out there and did the business. Like I say, we were determined to enjoy what was basically a new experience. And, of course, we knew that up there in the dressing-room everyone else was rooting for us. It's always been like that, ever since I've been at Lancashire. And down the years, Warren and I have earned a bit of a reputation for digging the side out of a hole. The Musketeers. We try to be positive. We always give it our best shot and if it doesn't come off, so be it. No one can blame us for not trying. I like to think the tradition we've built in the '90s will carry on right through the next decade when we finally decide it's time to call it a day.

That win over Middlesex was just one of so many magical memories. No wonder the Sunday League, in all its various shapes and sizes and different names, has always been a wee bit special for me. It gave me my Lancashire début in 1986, my first silverware two years later, another trophy in 1989, my county cap in 1990, a Lancashire record haul of 28 wickets in 1991 and two more titles in the last two seasons of the millennium. That's three Sunday championships, plus the Refuge Assurance Cup after winning the play-offs in 1988.

In the process, I've become something of a cult figure with the Old Trafford fans. They've always loved their Sunday cricket, and back in the early days were rewarded with the first two John Player League titles in 1969 and 1970. That was with the first great one-day side, which included magnificent performers like Clive and David Lloyd, Barry Wood, Farokh Engineer, Peter Lever, Jack Simmons, David Hughes and many more characters from Red Rose folklore.

Hughes and Simmo were still around, of course, when I first appeared on the scene with Warren. Chucky and I were very much the new kids on the block at first, with people like Simmo, Yozzer, Graeme Fowler and Paul Allott ranting and raving and panicking, pacing the dressing-room floor. All we could do was sit quietly in the corner with our heads down . . . trying desperately not to laugh. Nowadays, Warren and I are the ones who are calling everyone in sight while the kids sit around hoping we don't catch them laughing at us.

Jack Simmons was tremendously popular with the fans, particularly when he was nearing the end of his career in the late '80s. When he bowed out after our title success in 1989, the fans were looking for a successor. I fitted the bill perfectly. Same league background, same all-round skills – I hesitate to say same build, because Jack was always a bigger lad than I'll ever be! But we came from the same mould, and the supporters had singled me out as Simmo's heir apparent.

He was a big influence. I studied his approach and technique, talked to him about how to prepare for one-day and Championship cricket. He always used to say that as far as he was concerned, the two were basically no different. It was all about keeping it tight, bowling straight, frustrating the batsmen, forcing them into mistakes. That made a lot of sense. It still does.

Simmo was very much part of the set-up in the Championship and the one-dayers when we collected the first piece of silverware of my Lancashire career, the Refuge Cup in 1988. It was the first year that the end-of-season play-offs were tried, and for my money, it was a big success. The side finishing on top of the Sunday League were the champions and then the top four went into the hat for the play-offs, with another pot waiting at the end of the line.

We finished third and headed off down to Bristol to take on Gloucester. Good day, big crowd, a three-wicket win and a place in the final against Worcestershire, the champions, on a neutral ground at Edgbaston. The only fly in the ointment as far as our semi-final victory was concerned were the balls. As a bit of gimmick, the powers-that-be decided that for this competition, we would use bright orange balls which had a huge seam. They flew all over the place – I've never seen so much movement. No one could really control the swing, and if the umpires had stuck to the letter of the law, extras would have topped the 100 mark. Fortunately, they saw what was going on and the game finished before darkness fell.

The final was another big day and we got home by 52 runs, with Trevor Jesty making 59 and Winker 42. I took three 51 from 7.5 overs, including the last wicket – Richard Illingworth, caught by Warren for a duck. We made the play-offs in each of the next three seasons, finishing top of the table in '89 and second in '90 and '91. But that win in '88 was our only victory before they scrapped the play-off system for the 1992 season. A shame. It was like the football play-offs; they gave the final games of the Sunday League season a big lift, and those four finals were watched by around 40,000 fans.

As I say, the first outright Sunday League title I was involved in came along the following year. It went right down to the wire. Essex had led the way from the start of the season, but we pegged them back in the closing stages and when the final games came around, we knew that if we beat Surrey at Old Trafford the title was coming home in Simmo's last appearance for the county.

Surrey batted first and made 186. It should have been straightforward enough, but after Mendis and Fowler had put on 68 for the first wicket, we slipped away a bit. In fact, we slipped away a lot. When Paul Allott joined me out in the middle, we had slumped to 170 for seven.

But we kept it ticking over and at the start of the last over, we needed five. Walt was the senior man, so he led the mid-wicket discussion before the start of the over.

'Right, Oscar. We'll take our time. Don't do anything daft. Five runs, six balls. Field spread out. We can take it at a run a ball. Just keep calm . . .'

'OK, Walt.'

I retreated to the non-striker's end and waited for Martin Bicknell to bowl the first delivery. I was looking for Walt to run it down to third man or into one of the gaps on the off side, and was ready to scamper a single whatever happened. More or less.

On your marks, get set . . . Bicknell ran in and bowled. But instead of that cautious push for a single, Walt swung himself off his feet and the ball was still climbing as it whistled past my right ear. I put my head down and started to run. I needn't have bothered. When I looked up, Walt was running around like a whirling dervish, roughly in the direction of the pavilion, leaping up and down and waving his bat in the air. A big six over long on and to this day, I have no idea what happened to the ball. So much for not doing anything daft.

It was celebration time again, and a huge roar went up for Simmo when he came out on the pavilion balcony for the last time. He was one of the two players padded up and waiting to go in at the start of the last over and while the fans would have loved to see him hit the winning runs, I fancy Jack was happy to stay where he was.

In 1990, we finished runners-up to Derby and we were second

behind Notts in 1991. But this time there was the personal consolation for me of a new Sunday record for Lancashire of 28 wickets. I left it a bit late: after nine games I'd only taken 13 wickets. Then it all slotted into place and I took three for 40 against Somerset, three for 42 against Middlesex, one for 38 against Hampshire and four for 40 against Yorkshire. That set me up nicely for the final game against Gloucester down at Bristol, where I took four for 10 to overhaul Wasim's 1987 tally of 27. And all those four wickets came in the space of nine balls, at a cost of just two runs. Throw in that century stand with Chucky against Middlesex and you'll understand why 1991 was my Sunday best so far.

But we had to wait until 1998 before the name of Lancashire was inscribed on the Sunday trophy again. We finished third once, fourth twice and sixth in the next six seasons – and all of a sudden we were the nearly men, instead of the Sunday kings.

Why? It's hard to put a finger on it, but maybe it had something to do with killer instinct. Or the lack of it. We played in some great games; in fact time after time our matches went right down to the final over and on those occasions we were usually the side who came out on top when things got tight. In those situations we were still the great escape artists, but too often we found ourselves on the wrong end of the result against teams we should really have rolled over.

We sat down at the start of the 1998 season and talked it through. With two divisions on the agenda for 1999, the last thing we wanted was to finish out of the top nine. It had to be total commitment every week, never mind the strength of the opposition. And we got it right. That year we lost just twice in 17 matches and won the last one-division title by 12 points.

In 1999, under our new name of Lancashire Lightning, we started slowly and lost two games early on. We had to watch as Yorkshire Phoenix stormed off with five straight wins. And when the wheels came off for them, Worcester Royals took over at the top. But we were on a roll. In August, we beat Phoenix twice under floodlights in the space of a week and eventually cruised home with a bit to spare – our eighth one-day title of the decade, and the perfect way to end the old millennium.

Since I made my Sunday League début in 1986, the competition has had five different names and all sorts of different playing formats. We kicked off with the John Player League, 40 overs a side with bowlers off restricted run-ups. Then it became the Refuge Association League, the

AXA Equity and Law League, the CGU National League and now the Norwich Union National League. We've gone from 40 overs and short runs to 50 overs without run-up limits. And now it's down to 45 overs with fielding restrictions for the first 15, day-night games, team nicknames, coloured clothing, white balls and so on.

I don't really know why they've messed about with Sunday cricket so much. Basically, it was introduced simply as an entertainment. Forty overs a side, two o'clock start, all done and dusted by around 6.30 p.m. The traditionalists didn't like the idea, but a new generation of fans came along to see a few sixes hit, some spectacular fielding and plenty of wickets. It caught on in a big way and created a new audience for the game.

So why tinker with a winning formula? From talking to supporters, I reckon the current 45 overs format is just a shade too drawn out, a bit too much like the real thing if you like. I'd go back to 40 overs and I'd have no problems with restricting the bowlers' run-ups to ten paces or whatever. Coloured clothing? Definitely. Floodlights? A must. In fact, I'll never understand why pyjamas and day-night games weren't introduced much earlier.

When the World Cup was played under floodlights in Australia back in 1992, it was a huge success. That was the first time people in this country had seen day-night cricket, and there was an immediate demand for the same kind of thing over here, complete with coloured clothing. But what happened? Not a lot. Coloured clothing was introduced into the Sunday League in 1993 and supporters were given a chance to buy replica strips and wear their teams' colours. But floodlit cricket has only gradually forced its way on to the fixture list over the last three years. Why the hold-up? It's obviously the way to go for this particular competition. Not as a replacement for 'white' cricket, but as an alternative that will attract a newer, younger audience. Let's face it, they are the future of the game and if we don't catch them young, we'll lose them forever.

I've no objection to bouncy castles or rodeo bulls for the little ones to play on. They're never going to sit still for four or five hours, are they? So let them have a play if they want to, and give them a go at KwikCricket before the match and during the interval. Give the older ones a spell in the nets with a couple of professionals. Help them along the way with a bit of coaching. Make sure there are a few more players around to sign autographs.

I don't have a problem with burger stalls and ox roasts; I'll put up with a bit of music. And I love to see big crowds under the lights with the fans wearing their teams' colours. All the games in the National League should be day-night under permanent floodlights. Expensive? Yes. But so is hiring the lights on a one-off basis. Clubs would get their money back in the long term. They must be prepared to take a gamble and have the confidence to go out and make sure it pays off. And if people say it's not cricket, then my answer is that cricket is changing and must continue to change if it's going to survive. Yes, the day–night audience will be different from 'white' cricket, but if just a small percentage of the people who get their first taste of the game under the lights are still around in ten years, we'll be winning the battle.

There is plenty of room for improvement. The floodlights, for starters, which is why all the major grounds should have permanent lights. We just about get by with the temporary lights, but they are nowhere near as good as the set-up in Australia and South Africa where lights have been installed at the big venues.

Our first day-night venture at Old Trafford was a challenge match against Yorkshire, the old enemy, three years ago. It was very much a dry run for the real thing and billed as a family night out. The innings were split into four sections of 25 overs with Yorkshire batting last under the lights. They looked to be home and dry until they lost four wickets in five balls and went down by 13 runs. I had a chat with some of their players afterwards and they told me that they just couldn't really see the ball. I know I wouldn't have fancied having a bat under those conditions in a game that really mattered.

Things have improved since that experimental stage, but we should aim at introducing permanent lights, and in this country, Sussex have set an example that we should all be following.

That Yorkshire game also featured live interviews with players as they returned to the pavilion after getting out. It was a bit of fun. But I dread to think what might have happened if it had been a serious game and not just a showpiece. OK, it happens in football, but there's a world of difference between the two sports. In football, all the players leave the field together at the final whistle and the interviewer can be selective. He invariably goes for the man of the match – and not the goalkeeper whose just thrown in two in the last five minutes, because he knows what the answer will be: short, sharp, rude and probably no more than two words. He would get the same answer if he shoved a microphone at a batsman who'd just sacrificed himself in a run-out with the game going right down to the wire. Family entertainment? I think not! It's a risky business, and if we're going down that track, it would require a very experienced and sensitive interviewer to handle it properly.

We haven't got it right out in the middle, either. We must retain a balance between bat and ball. Entertain the fans, by all means. But let's not forget we're playing a game of cricket for a trophy and prize money, and we need to give the bowlers a fair crack of the whip. As a bowler, I would say that, wouldn't I? But the bottom line is that we are still trying to look to the future of English cricket, and would-be bowlers aren't going to get much encouragement from watching the one-day game in its current form: we're tinkering with the rules purely for the sake of entertainment.

Take this free hit nonsense. A bowler will always bowl no-balls and the laws of the game state that his side must be penalised. You accept that. But why should it be two for the no-ball, plus whatever the batsman scores – and then a free hit on top next ball? It's just a cheap gimmick, and it's the same with this wides business. You stray down the leg side, the keeper misses it, and the batting side collects two for the wide ball, four for the boundary and an extra ball on top.

And what about bumpers? They are a vital part of a quick bowler's armoury in any class of cricket. But at the moment, in one-day matches anything above shoulder height is called a no-ball. Why? I haven't yet met a top-quality batsman who would object to one bumper an over. It's all part and parcel of the game. But instead, any Tom, Dick or Harry can come in knowing that he's got a licence to swing from the hip and there's not a lot the bowler can do about it in retaliation. But put one round their earholes to let 'em know you've got something in the locker too, and it's a no-ball.

We have to dangle a carrot in front of young players to encourage them to concentrate on their bowling. The last thing we want is for the next generation to come to cricket believing that it's a batsman's game and the bowlers are just there to supply a bit of cannon fodder.

All in all, though, we're on the right track. And as long as the authorities are prepared to listen to the feedback from the players as well as the marketing men, I'm certain that floodlit cricket will be a winner.

6
A BED OF ROSES

Friday, 6 September 1991. Scarborough. Lancashire, chasing 343, are reduced to 129 for eight as Yorkshire coast towards a Roses victory over the old enemy in front of a near full-house at the Scarborough Cricket Festival. Enter Austin. In only his second Roses innings, he hammers the fastest century of the season and, for a while at least, the match is no longer a foregone conclusion. His love affair with Roses cricket has begun.

Who says Roses cricket doesn't matter any more? Not me, for one. Not the boys in the Lancashire dressing-room, either. And I'm 100 per cent certain that if you asked any of the Yorkies, they'd say the old passion is still burning just as strongly in White Rose territory, too.

The days are long gone when the two Roses matches in the County Championship meant the 'house full' notices went out a couple of hours before play began at Old Trafford, Headingley or Bramall Lane. But those two games against Yorkshire are still the ones we want to win more than any other. Or to put it another way, they're the ones we desperately don't want to lose. If we do, it's guaranteed that the stick will fly the next time any of the players pop into the local for what they hoped would be a quiet pint.

These are still the first games supporters look for when the fixture lists come out. If the two sides are drawn against one another in one of the big one-day competitions, the bus hire companies can stand by for some overtime. And while the Championship games might not have such a high profile these days, you can guarantee that any one-day match between the sides will attract a near-capacity crowd.

In my time, we've had some fantastic one-day games against Yorkshire, both in the two major trophies and in the Sunday League. In day-night games, once again, the atmosphere is terrific. I won't rub salt into White Rose wounds by reminding them of our two semi-final victories at Old Trafford back in 1996. Not just yet, anyway!

My Roses début in the Championship came at Old Trafford back in August, 1990. It was a draw. Athers and Winker scored hundreds for us and my contribution was 21 and four overs for five runs. A modest start.

It was a different story when I came face-to-face with Yorkshire again at Scarborough the following September. It was the feature match at the Scarborough Festival, so there were decent crowds on all four days. The game was played on one of those old-fashioned North Marine Road shirt fronts and for three days, the batters filled their boots. David Byas, Phil Robinson and Martyn Moxon hit tons for Yorkshire and Gehan Mendis replied for us before Moxon made the third declaration of the match and set us a target of 343 in 80 overs. At 99 for seven, things didn't look too promising.

In reality, we had more or less given the game up. Before he went out to bat at the fall of the fifth wicket, Phil DeFreitas turned to me and said: 'Right, Bully, let's see who can hit the quickest fifty.' He put down a pretty good marker, posting his half century off just 28 balls, but when he was eighth out on 129 we were still a million miles away. We crossed as I went out to bat. 'OK, that's what you've got to beat,' said Daffy. Fair enough.

Darren Gough had made the early breakthrough for Yorkshire, but good old Phil Carrick had been twirling away with his left-arm spinners from the Pavilion End for some time when I arrived at the crease and had already been on the receiving end of a battering from Daffy. Things didn't get any better with me around.

It should have been a left-hander's nightmare. Carrick was a very useful bowler and was landing it in the foot-holes on the line of the off stump. I was surrounded by close catchers. There was variable bounce and basically, batting was a lottery. There was no point defending. No point at all. I decided I was going to play a few shots. If I was going to get out, so be it. I wouldn't get out wondering, as they say. So I started swinging from the word go and clubbed a couple of sixes straight away.

Carrick, or Fergie as he was universally known, was a good lad and didn't mind a laugh and a joke about it at first. He knew it was only a matter of time; Moxon knew it was only a matter of time; the Yorkshire players knew it was only a matter of time; the Scarborough fans, relishing the prospect of a heavy Lancashire defeat, knew it was only a matter of time. So, they thought, if some kid wants to come in and entertain us for 20 minutes, fair enough. Let's enjoy it while it lasts. Carrick and Moxon were working on the theory that I wouldn't be able to keep hitting it as cleanly as I was. Eventually, I was bound to hole out. They started to send a few scouts out to the boundary – a man at deep square, another at mid-wicket, another at long-on. But I kept hitting them over the top and the sixes and the fours kept coming.

Dexter Fitton was batting at the other end and decided to join in the fun. Good player, Dex, but never your most orthodox performer. And when he started hitting Fergie against the spin, it was too much. 'Fucking hell, not another one,' he groaned, as Fitton started to match me shot for shot.

By the time we'd put on 83 in 11 overs for the ninth wicket and I'd beaten Daffy's target, the natives were getting distinctly restless. Cries of 'Rubbish, Carrick!' and 'Get 'im off, Moxon!' rang out all around the ground. But still Fergie wouldn't give up. The breakthrough came when Dexter got out with the score on 212. I was in the eighties by this time, and normal service was resumed among the Yorkshire players and supporters.

Pete Martin was last man. Now there are many, many worse number elevens around than Digger, but I could tell as he walked out that he was as nervous as a kitten. I couldn't work it out.

'What's up, Pete?'

'I just don't want to get out, Bully, that's all. Not with you so near your first ton. So come on, get on with it.'

Get on with it? What did he think I'd been doing before he emerged from the pavilion? That little exchange ended up making me nervous as well, as I realised how close I was. Instead of blasting away, I started pottering around a bit although Digger was straight in the groove, with 26 off a single over from poor old Carrick. I finally reached the three figures just before tea. Sixty-one balls, 68 minutes, six sixes and 13 fours. It beat Matthew Maynard's previous best of the season by 14 balls and to be fair to the Yorkshire fans, they gave me a hell of a reception.

Carrick had finally taken a breather by this stage, but me and Pete had already pushed it well past 250 and it suddenly dawned on us that we could just win it. Fatal!

The tea interval came at exactly the wrong time. We lost some of our adrenaline, and Yorkshire had a chance to regroup. And it didn't help that in the dressing-room the rest of the lads kept saying: 'Come on boys, we can nick this one. They're rattled.' We had a chance to work out a strategy instead of just blazing away and sure enough, straight after the interval, Pete had a flash at one outside off stump and got a nick, thanks very much and away you go. Caught Moxon, bowled Peter Hartley 29. I was left unbeaten on 101. It must have been great stuff for the neutrals and, eventually, the Yorkshire fans. The next day, I hogged my fair share of the headlines.

I enjoyed every minute of it, of course, but the bottom line is we still lost the game. Would I rather have got a duck and Lancashire win the game? There's no answer to that! But deep down, I know the team always comes first.

I had a drink afterwards with Fergie. He was laughing and joking about it. Correction: I was laughing and joking, Fergie was cursing and swearing!

As luck would have it, we were back at Scarborough the following season and once again, there was Fergie waiting for me when I went out to bat. 'Bloody 'ell, not you again!' he said through gritted teeth. Second ball, down the track, over the top. Six. I really middled the next ball again, straight back at him. Fergie instinctively stuck out a hand and the ball caught him right on the end of the finger. He took one look at me and said: 'Right, that'll do for me. I've had enough. I'm not carrying on where we left off last year.' Claiming he couldn't grip the ball any more, he was removed from the attack. We always had a laugh about that down the years. He was a lovely man. What a terrible tragedy he passed away so young.

That match set a pattern for many of the Roses games I have been involved in since then. Usually they have been close. One team has looked out of it then clawed its way back, or else it has gone right down to the wire. And never more so than in those epic one-day matches in the mid-'70s.

The first was a NatWest quarter-final at Headingley in 1995. This was the game that introduced us to Michael Bevan. It was his first season with Yorkshire and at that stage he was relatively unknown outside Australia – and the Lancashire League. He'd played for Rawtenstall for a couple of seasons before signing for Yorkshire, and made a huge impression. Bevan has gone on to become recognised as one of the best one-day batters in the world and he will always back himself to win a match, however dodgy the situation. That's what he did at Headingley in 1995. He took it upon himself to steer Yorkshire to victory, but I will always maintain that he came within a whisker of steering them down the pan.

It was a low-scoring affair. We made 169 but apart from Bevan and, late in the innings, Ashley Metcalfe, Yorkshire lost wickets regularly, too. They were never quite up with the asking rate and needed something like 16 off the last two overs. Bevan decided to take on Glenn Chapple in the 49th, and he went for ten or 12. Yorkshire got home by two wickets with three balls to spare. But it needn't have been that close and if some of those shots had hit the fielders, they wouldn't have made it. In the end, Bevan played a matchwinning innings, a tremendous knock. But if he had got out near the death there was no one who could have picked up the striking rate in the same way. That's his style, and on this occasion, it paid off.

Bevan threatened to take us to the cleaners again the following year at Old Trafford, this time in a Benson & Hedges semi-final, a game that will go down as one of the all-time one-day classics. There was a delayed start and Yorkshire were right in the mire at 83 for five when Dick Blakey joined Bevan. They added 115 before the close and then hammered us for another 52 from the last four overs the next morning. At 97 for five, chasing 251, there looked to be no way back for us. Or that's what everyone on the ground thought, except Warren Hegg. He hit a magnificent 81 and when he was out, the target was down to 11 off 13 balls. That became eight off Craig White's last over and Glenn Chapple and Peter Martin somehow scrambled through off the last ball.

We got out of jail all right. But in the end, it might all have been down to Yorkshire's decision to change the ball late in our innings. The old one had gone a bit soft, and they asked the umpires for another one. We couldn't believe it. Our batters were having trouble getting the old ball away but as soon as the new one arrived, it started to fly off the bat much quicker and those few extra runs were almost certainly decisive. It was champagne all round in the home dressing-room. Yorkshire, apparently, were absolutely devastated.

There was another ball change when we met them again later that year in the semi-final of the NatWest. Once again, Old Trafford was the venue, with Yorkshire looking to become the first team to beat us in a home tie in the NatWest since 1987. I don't think I've ever seen a side so fired up. Apparently they had team meeting after team meeting preparing for the match, but we just rolled up as normal on the morning of the game. Just another match, lads.

We've never gone in for team meetings. Call it arrogance if you like, but we reckon that if we play up to our potential, we can beat anyone. So we don't worry about what the opposition may or may not do. We concentrate on our own game, knowing that if every individual performs, we will win.

We were in the driving seat from the start. Graham Lloyd hit 81 as we posted 293 for nine and it was always going to be too many, even with Bevan around. And it didn't help Yorkshire that the ball went soft again. It was like a pudding and the batsmen kept complaining about it to the umpires, asking for a change. They offered it to us and we said play on. We were bowling OK with it, and if Yorkshire couldn't get the ball off the square that was their problem. In the end, Bevan solved the issue with a cover drive that saw one half of the ball fly on the offside and the other towards mid-on. What would have happened if someone had caught one of the two halves is anyone's guess.

The replacement suited me down to the ground. In the space of nine balls, I removed Bevan for 85, Craig White first ball, Anthony McGrath for 34 and we were on our way to Lord's for the second time that season. Oh, and thanks for the Man of the Match award. Within minutes of the game ending, a helicopter landed on the ground, Bevan leaped in and was flown off to Heathrow to link up with Australia for a tour of Sri Lanka. No doubt he was heartily glad to see the back of us for another season.

Yorkshire finally broke our stranglehold in 1999, winning a NatWest quarter-final with a bit to spare. They outplayed us in every department. Simple as that, and we held our hands up and said as much afterwards. They had waited a long time to beat us and they played tremendously well on the day. Before that game, there was always the suspicion that they allowed negative thoughts to creep in when they played us at our place. But not that time. Our performance didn't help – and if we needed a kick up the backside, Yorkshire provided it big time. Five days later they took on Gloucester in the Benson & Hedges Super Cup final at Lord's and blew it badly. Why? On paper, Yorkshire are a tremendous side and they had just rolled us over at Old Trafford. They were overwhelming favourites. Perhaps they thought that after beating us so convincingly they had done the hard bit and it was downhill from there. Or perhaps, deep down, they didn't really believe they could do it. Who knows. But once a side earns a reputation for bottling it on the big occasion, it's bound to take a toll psychologically.

At the risk of upsetting the Red Rose fraternity, I was rooting for Yorkshire down at Lord's. All I'm interested in is winning trophies for Lancashire. But if it isn't going to be our turn, I'd rather see Yorkshire win than anyone else. We're closer to their players than any other side in the Championship: we've more or less grown up together, either as opponents or playing in the same regional sides. We still tend to stick together when we play at international level. It's not exactly a North-South divide, but if there's a game of soccer or whatever in training, it will usually be North v South. Basically, we've always played our cricket in the same way.

That's why Roses cricket is still important and even in this day and age, the Roses match is the one Championship fixture that will ensure a big crowd if both sides happen to be in contention for the trophy, particularly now that we have two divisions. Sadly, though, we won't be meeting them in the National League this season. With three up and three down, there's precious little margin for error and I suppose it was inevitable that sooner or later one of us would find ourselves in the wrong division. Unfortunately it was sooner, not later – and it was Lancashire. Losing those two games from the fixture list will take a big chunk out of everyone's season – players and supporters on both sides of the Pennines. Hopefully, normal service will be resumed in 2002. In Division One, of course!

Saturday, 14 July, 1990. Benson & Hedges Final, Lancashire 241 for eight, Worcestershire 172, a winning start in Austin's first one-day final. He is not to know there will be seven more before the end of the decade.

We've got it down to a fine art now. A ritual, if you like. But that first time, it was a whole new experience for most of us. David Hughes, Graeme Fowler, Neil Fairbrother, Mike Watkinson and Paul Allott survived from the last Lancashire side to play in a Lord's final, the 1984 victory over Warwickshire. But for the rest of us, the build-up to that final against Worcester set the precedent for all those other trips to Lord's that were to follow in the next nine years.

It starts as soon as we win the semi-final. A couple of days later, the tailors arrive and we're measured up for our new suits and shirts. There are new ties and new shoes as well. We travel down to London by coach first thing in the morning on the day before the game. We call in at Lord's to leave our kit, sort out the dressing-room and generally get the feel of the old place. Then we check in at the Hilton International, just a couple of minutes' walk from the main gates.

The wives, girlfriends, families and the rest of the official party come down on the train later in the day and join us in the hotel. It's a weekend off for the ladies, too. We spend a lot of time socialising together and they all get on pretty well. They do a bit of phoning around in advance. Someone is in charge of the Pimms, someone else the lemonade, someone else the bread sticks and so on. They all go out on the town on the night before the match while we take it easy. We're encouraged to do our own thing. For some of the boys, that means room service, one or two eat in the hotel, some like to have a pub meal or go for an Indian or a Chinese. There's a good Thai restaurant a few streets away. Others might go for a bite to eat with their parents or families. It's all very relaxed and informal. I like to have a couple of pints in the pub and then probably a Chinese before a reasonably early night.

We have a private room for breakfast and there's always a box of red roses waiting for us, ready to be pinned on to our suits. We walk across to the ground as the fans are already starting to gather, get changed, warm up . . . and away we go. To start with we always preferred the away dressing-room because that's what we were used to. But one year we were given the home dressing-room and we still won, so now there are no particular superstitions on that score. After the game, win or lose, we have a night out together, usually at Stringfellows, which makes a big dent in the players' pool! Then we nurse our hangovers back up the M6. The girls are with us on the coach this time.

By and large, that's been the batting order for just about every one of my Lord's finals, although there have been exceptions. One year, we travelled down two or three days before the game and the plan was to have a day's golf on the Thursday, a net on the morning before the match and then an afternoon off. The idea was that the longer build-up would relax us a bit. As it happened, it pissed down with rain all morning so we missed out on the net session and found ourselves hanging around with nothing to do in the afternoon. The build-up seemed endless. I ended up going to my room and having a kip, sleeping for about four hours. Result? I couldn't get to sleep that night.

It was getting on for midnight and I was tossing and turning so, rather than stay in my room, I decided to get dressed and nip down to the bar; see if there was anyone around to talk to. I bought a couple of orange juices and chatted to a few supporters. After a while I went back upstairs and got off to sleep.

A couple of days later, all hell broke loose. I was summoned before the hierarchy and hauled over the coals. They asked me what I thought I was doing in the bar in the early hours on the night before a Lord's final. I explained what had happened, and in the end I got away with it. But it had been a close call, and I've stayed in my room ever since. It seems the secret is to be seen to be doing the right thing – even if it's the wrong thing for the player concerned.

Basically, though, we try to treat Lord's like any other game. If your scene back home is to pop down to the pub for a couple of pints and then have a curry on the night before a game, then that's what you do at Lord's. Follow the usual routine and there's no reason why you won't perform. It all came as a bit of a shock to Andy Flintoff in his first Lord's final a couple of years ago, though. Soon after we arrived at the hotel, I asked him if he fancied joining me and Graham Lloyd for a pint and a bite to eat that night. He looked at me as if I'd come from another planet: 'But we're supposed to be playing in a Lord's final tomorrow. We can't go out tonight.'

'Look, Flinty. If you were at home right now, what would you be doing? Answer: going out for a pint and something to eat. So why do anything different because we happen to be playing at Lord's tomorrow?'

The trouble was, when we set out for the pub just round the corner from the hotel it started to rain and, by the time we arrived, it was absolutely pelting down. The plan was to move on after a couple of beers but when we poked our noses out of the front door, it was still bouncing down outside. So we had a meal in the pub and sure enough, when we decided to set off back to the hotel at about 10.30 p.m., the rain was still lashing down.

Outside the pub there were a few tables for summer drinking, complete with great big striped umbrellas. We'll just have one of these for starters,' said Andy. 'Oh no you won't,' I replied as he started to manhandle one of the brollies out of its socket. 'Not unless you want to spend the night in the bloody nick. Excuse me, officer, can I go now? I'm playing in a Lord's final in half an hour. The press boys would have had a field day with that one.'

Flinty took the point. So we decided the only alternative was to leg it back to the hotel as fast as we could. I got my head down and ran like a bat out of hell. Now with the best will in the world, I'm not the quickest. And over 200 yards I fully expected Bumble to show me a clean pair of heels, even if I might see Flinty off with a bit of luck. But instead, I claimed the gold medal as I breasted the finishing tape and charged into the hotel lobby. I was soaked to the skin – and somewhat surprised to find no evidence of any pursuers.

After a couple of minutes, Lloyd and Flintoff came strolling into the foyer, sheltering under a couple of dustbin lids they'd 'borrowed' from an alley beside the pub. And yes, they were taken back the following morning.

Of course, all that happened eight years down the road from my own first final in the Benson & Hedges Cup against Worcester in 1990. To be honest, I can't remember too much about it. The whole thing flew by in a blur. We batted first, lost a couple of early wickets before Athers and Winker both scored runs. That was the platform for Wasim to come in and change the course of the game – with bat and ball. He hammered a quickfire 28 off 33 balls with two massive sixes that gave the run rate the injection we needed. The tail chipped in and we finished up with 241 for eight.

Then Waz the bowler took over. He was bloody quick that day. Really fired up. He came on first change and got rid of Tim Curtis straight away and then had Graeme Hick caught behind for one. We were on our way. Botham looked dangerous for a while, but after he went for 38 there was only going to be one winner. I picked up Phil Neale for nought and Stuart Lampitt at the death to finish with two for 44. I'd been on a real high from the moment I woke up and the adrenaline was working overtime for the next 12 hours. I changed next to Waz and I could sense he felt exactly the same. It was his first Lord's final, too, and like me he didn't know whether he would ever be going back. We weren't going to miss out.

At the end, we slumped down on the bench in the corner and looked at one another. We didn't need to speak: our expressions said it all. We were both absolutely knackered, completely drained. For a few minutes, no one really said anything. Then the first champagne cork popped, the cup was filled with all sorts of horrendous concoctions and the celebrations began in earnest. It's incredible how a few glasses of bubbly can revive a tired cricketer!

But like I say, my memories of the actual occasion are pretty vague. I was so engrossed in the action that I never noticed the crowd, the noise or the atmosphere. I think most of the lads felt the same. Thankfully, we had a chance to put the record straight less than two months later when we went back to Lord's to take on Northants in the final of the NatWest Trophy. We were looking to become the first team to do the one-day double and Yozzer was in the frame to add a NatWest winners' medal to the five Gillette medals he had picked up with the all-conquering team of the '60s.

Allan Lamb did us a kingsize favour by losing the toss, Yozzer put them in and Phil DeFreitas won the match in the first hour by ripping out their first five batsmen for 15 runs in 35 balls. Curtly Ambrose hammered 48 down the order, but their total of 171 from 60 overs was never going to be enough and we won it by three wickets with 14 overs to spare. This time, thanks to Daffy's early breakthrough, we knew we were on a winner early in the game and there was a chance to savour the atmosphere of a Lord's final. A full house at the most famous cricket ground in the world. The tension before the start, the roar as the players take the field from fans who have made the journey to London looking for a really good day out. It's a unique atmosphere and I realise exactly how lucky I have been to sample it in eight finals. As Hartley Alleyne predicted all those years ago, cricket has given me some marvellous memories.

We lost out to Worcester by 65 runs in the Benson final the following year and in 1993 Derbyshire edged us out by six runs, also in the Benson. Both games went into a second day and while Worcester beat us fair and square, I'm convinced the weather played a part in the Derby match. They made 252 for six, with Dominic Cork getting 92 and Karl Krikken knocking it around a bit at the end. But Athers, Nick Speak and Neil Fairbrother had pushed us past the 150 mark before the rain came down and we had to start all over again the next day. The momentum had gone and even though Harvey finished with 87 not out off 85 balls, we never quite got it back.

It was a big disappointment, and defeat made us all the more determined not to be rolled over three times in a row when we went back to Lord's for the Benson final in 1995. It was a game that featured just about the best one-day innings I have ever seen from the master himself, Aravinda da Silva. Athers made 93 and John Crawley 83 as we posted 274 for seven from our 55 overs. Glenn Chapple took a couple of quick wickets at the start of their innings and they were on the back foot. Enter Da Silva. He hammered us for 112 from 95 balls with three sixes and eleven fours. It was wonderful stuff – unless you happened to be on the receiving end. And while he was at the crease, Kent were winning the match. He carried them from 37 for two to 214 for seven before I finally persuaded him to hole out to Bumble on the square leg boundary. That was the end of the opposition and we eased in by 35 runs.

I had no complaints about Aravinda claiming the Man of the Match award, even though we won the game. It's a bit of a thing with me normally, though. I can't really come to terms with someone from the losing side picking up the award. They might have batted or bowled well, but their team has still lost.

That happens a lot in the early rounds of the NatWest when a first-class county plays one of the minor counties. The first-class boys usually win, and one of the batters will make a ton or one of the bowlers pick up a five-for or better. Then what happens? The award goes to a minor counties player who has made a defiant half century or picked up a few wickets. It's a sympathy vote, I suppose. But as a professional, I like to see the game's most effective performer collect the award. I certainly wouldn't like to lift the Man of the Match award in a losing side. It's all about winning, and you get nowt for coming second.

However I had to make an exception in Aravinda's case, for what was certainly one of the finest innings played in a Lord's final. Yet I will always maintain I should have had him caught on the square leg boundary 112 runs earlier. When he came in, I'd already bowled my first three overs: three maidens. I felt pretty confident. I always have a game plan worked out in advance, which features an orthodox deep square leg right on the boundary. That's what I wanted when Aravinda arrived at the crease.

But Winker and Athers had other ideas. They thought that because Da Silva is such a wristy player, the man at square leg should be pushed 10 or 15 yards behind square rather than in the position I wanted. I'd been around for seven or eight years by that time and reckoned I knew what was best for me. I still do. So I argued my case strongly that I'd never had a fielder there before, so why start now, Da Silva or no Da Silva? But in the end, the views of the Lancashire captain and the England captain prevailed.

Sure enough, two balls later, Aravinda clipped me over square leg for six. The ball landed about a yard over the rope, exactly where my fielder would have been. Anyone out there who could lip read would have had no trouble in working out my reaction. Just to prove it wasn't a fluke, he did it again a couple of balls later, and this time he must have made a better connection because the ball landed about 15 rows back. Then he cut me through point for four.

All three shots were featured on the evening highlights on the box and for weeks people kept coming up to me and saying: 'Bloody hell, Oscar, that Da Silva bloke didn't half give you some stick at Lord's. It's a good job you got him in the end.' My figures? Eleven overs, four maidens, 36 runs, two wickets. And Aravinda hit me for 20 of them off four balls. It just goes to show: never believe what you see on the highlights!

But that near miss puts the spotlight on a major issue: who decides on the field – bowler or captain? It won't surprise anyone when I say that as a bowler, I always want to be able to set my own field. I've been around long enough to know what I want. If it doesn't work out, fair enough – the skipper has every right to say I told you so. But bowlers run on confidence and if there is a bit of a niggle in the back of your mind about the field placings, there will also be an element of doubt. Your performance will suffer.

I put my money where my mouth is when I captained the Sunshine Coast and Maroochydore out in Queensland. I said to the bowlers: 'Right, set your field. And if it doesn't work out, I'll come and have a word in a few overs.' I haven't had much more captaincy experience down the years, but if the chance comes along again, that's how I'll play it.

In the end, Aravinda played the major role in a memorable final that could have gone either way. But I would have been very frustrated, to put it mildly, if we had missed out. As it was, that win over Kent was the start of four straight wins at headquarters, starting with the Benson final against Northants the following year. A game Curtly Ambrose constantly reminds me about. We batted first and had reached 236 for seven when I went in. Curtly had just come on for his last few overs. I'd moved on to 18 when Curtly pitched one well up – and you don't come across many of those from him. I really laid into it. It was just about the hardest I've ever hit a cricket ball, and it was straight back at Curtly. There was no way he could get out of the way, so he stuck out a huge right hand and the ball went straight in. And stayed there.

Curtly didn't know whether to laugh or cry. Neither did I, for that matter, as I watched him hopping around. Three months later, we played down at Northants and after the warm-up on the first day I ambled over for a word with Curtly. I tried to shake hands. 'No way, man, hand still too sore!' Our total of 245 for nine gave us plenty to defend and I picked up a couple of early wickets and two more late on to finish with four for 21 from 9.3 overs and my first Man of the Match award in a Lord's final.

The 1996 NatWest final was against Essex. We never quite got going with the bat, although we still reckoned our total of 186 would be just about enough. But as we left the dressing-room, we knew we'd have to keep it very tight against a batting line-up featuring men like Graham Gooch, Nasser Hussain and Ronnie Irani.

Peter Willey was one of the umpires and very early on I caught Goochie absolutely plumb in front as the ball hit the pad. It would have knocked out all three. Even Goochie knew his fate and had started to make his move for the pavilion as all the close fielders went up. 'Not out,' said Willey. Not out? I couldn't believe it. I finished the over and as I went to collect my cap and sweater, the re-run of the incident was being shown on the giant screen. It was greeted with a groan from the Lancashire fans and a roar of delight from the Essex section. Peter was watching it, too. He gave me a wry smile. 'I think I might just owe you one there, Oscar,' he said.

'Too bloody right, Will!'

And if you're reading this, Peter, I'm still waiting for the payback! But to be fair, umpires only have a split second to make a decision and quite honestly, it's a case of you win some, you lose some. John Crawley had got away with a similar near miss in our innings so this one evened it up a bit.

I think I probably bowled better in that final than in any of my Lord's appearances. Yet by the time we had wiped Essex out for 57 to win by 129 runs, my figures were nought for ten from seven overs. Perhaps if Will had given me the benefit of no doubt at all I might have gone on to collect a few wickets but as it was, Glenn Chapple earned the Man of the Match prize with figures of six for 18 from 6.2 overs, the best analysis in a Lord's final and figures that will take a bit of beating.

There were comments in the press afterwards that the final had been a damp squib. Perhaps so, but don't blame the players. We go out there to do a job and on that particular occasion, Lancashire used the conditions to our advantage and did it damn well. It wasn't our fault that the game was the shortest final on record, finishing at 5.26 p.m. Of course, supporters want a nailbiter, they want to see the match go down to the last ball. But you can't plan these things. They just happen. So how do the players feel about it? Would we rather dish out a hammering or go right down to the wire? It's a difficult one. There's no better feeling than winning a real close one! It's thrilling for the players as well as the fans. But I fancy 95 per cent would rather give the opposition a hiding and collect the trophy and the winners' cheque the easy way.

It was another easy one when we made our final appearance of the decade in the 1998 NatWest final. Derbyshire again. Rain delayed the start until 4.30, but after we had won the toss and stuck them in, we didn't have a lot of luck against Michael Slater and Kim Barnett early doors. They put on 70 for the first wicket before Wasim, our skipper that year, introduced his secret weapon. Me.

For years I'd opened the bowling in the one-dayers and then come back at the death. In the process, I'd built up a reputation as being one of the best 'death' bowlers in the game. It's all about having a game plan. And there's no substitute for experience. I like to think when I come back for those last few overs that I've got it all worked out; I know my options. If Plan A isn't working, switch to Plan B. And afterwards, if the game has been on telly, I always have a long, hard look at the video, see where I went right and, more importantly, what went wrong, then put it all in the memory bank and prepare for the next time. But the bottom line is that you have to be ready to back yourself to do it. You have to be confident. If not, you might as well not bother.

For that last final, though, we had a change of plan. Waz and Pete Martin would open up, with Glenn first change and me at number four. I bowled from the pavilion end. It was doing a bit. My first over was reasonably tight. I got Slater leg before in my second and bowled through from there. I removed Robin Weston for nought, Matthew Cassar for six and finished with three for 14 from my ten overs. And four of them were overthrows.

It was good enough to earn me my second Man of the Match award – a gold medal plus a cheque for what turned out to be an unknown sum. I caught a brief glimpse of the paperwork before it was removed from my grasp and deposited in the players' pool. I've no problems with that. The Man of the Match prize is a nice little bonus, nothing more. I never go into one-day games thinking I might come away with the award. It never even enters my mind. I just hope I can contribute to the team effort. But to win a Lord's final, collect the award and earn an England call-up in the space of three weeks was one hell of a way to end the 1998 season. And to cap it all, I was later named as one of *Wisden's* five cricketers of the year. It doesn't get much better than that.

8
ENGLAND MY ENGLAND

17 August, 1998. Lancashire are playing Yorkshire at Headingley. A telephone call comes through for Dav Whatmore, their coach. From David Graveney, Chairman of the England Selectors. Austin has been called up by England for the Emirates Tournament, a one-day series also involving Sri Lanka and South Africa.

Me, play for England? I couldn't believe it. An England cap had never been on the agenda. Until Hartley Alleyne knocked some sense into me at Haslingden, I'd never even thought about playing for Lancashire, let alone England.

There are some players who seem destined to represent their country from the moment they hold a bat. Others are marked down at an early age and gradually climb the ladder until the call comes. And there are those who force their way into contention by high-class county performances. I had always been seen as just a good county pro. And I had no problems with that. Once or twice, there had been whispers that I might be not a million miles away from the England one-day line-up. In fact, when David Lloyd was coach at Lancashire, he was so incensed about one England squad that he sat down and wrote to the Chairman of Selectors, demanding five changes. I was one of them. I don't think Bumble even got a reply.

So you'll see why, when we started the Roses Match at Headingley in August 1998, my thoughts were a million miles away from an England call-up. At 32, my time had probably gone – and that Headingley track looked full of runs. It was a good toss to win and we racked up 455 for eight on the first day. I made 49.

Afterwards, we hung around to watch Leeds Rhinos in the Super League and then we all went for a bite to eat and a couple of beers. Iestyn Harris, the Leeds Rugby League skipper and a good mate of one or two of the Lancashire players, came into the bar soon afterwards with a few of his colleagues. One thing led to another, and by the time play started the next morning, a handful of our boys were thinking in terms of a nice quiet morning in the dressing-room while we added to our overnight score. Instead, Yorkshire rolled us out in no time at all and we found ourselves in the field after about half an hour.

We were without Waz, who was back in his hotel room feeling unwell. So I opened the bowling. It was obviously going to be a long day because the wicket still wasn't doing a lot. After bowling about seven overs, I was trudging back to third man when I saw Dav Whatmore, our coach, running round the boundary towards me with a big smile on his face. I couldn't work it out.

'Congratulations, Bully. You've been called into the England squad. You've got to go down to Lord's. Stop on 'til lunchtime, and then set off down this afternoon.'

Now there's never been a shortage of wind-up artists in the Lancashire dressing-room, and I had every reason to reckon I was on the receiving end in a big way this time. I looked round to see how many of the boys were trying not to laugh and to find out who was behind this particular plot, no doubt hatched over a beer the night before. But no one seemed to be taking much interest. And Dav insisted it was all above board. Lord's had been on the phone. I was in the squad.

Word gradually filtered through to the rest of the lads and, one by one, they came over and shook my hand. The Yorkshire batsmen said well done, too. Then it was announced over the PA system that Ian Austin had been called up by England. 'And I'm sure you will all want to join me in wishing him all the very best in the triangular series with South Africa and Sri Lanka.' I decided that this was either the biggest wind-up of all time, with a cast of thousands, or I really had been chosen by England. I still couldn't be sure. But a couple of committee men came round and congratulated me and then one of the press boys asked if I could spare them a few minutes at lunchtime. It slowly dawned on me that it was true. I was going to play for England against

Sri Lanka at Lord's less than 24 hours later. Mark Ealham had been forced to drop out of the squad of 15 for the Emirates Tournament, and I was the replacement.

I was in a bit of a daze from then on. I came off at lunch, spoke to the press for a while and then rang home. Alex already knew because Graeme Fowler had picked up the news and called her straight away. So I told her to drop everything and get on the next train to London. Then I rang my Mum and Dad. Mum hadn't heard and was about as stunned as me and twice as happy, if that was possible. I told her to tell Dad so they could arrange to be down at Lord's as well. She said I could call in and tell him myself on the way down: he was at Chesterfield, watching Burnley.

As it happened, some of his mates had heard the news and when they bumped into him at the match, they told him I'd been called up. Being a true Claret, he stayed around for the full 90 minutes then left the ground at the final whistle, drove home, collected Mum and the cases then turned straight round and set off down to London.

It should have been all go for me, too. I packed my bags and loaded up the car, said cheerio to the lads, moved in behind the wheel, switched on the ignition . . . and two men in suits appeared in my wing mirrors. One of them knocked on the window. 'You can't set off yet. We need to have a word.' I thought I'd been arrested. In fact, it was the random drug test team. I couldn't leave the ground until I'd given them a sample. A tricky one. The rules state that anyone playing in a game has to give a sample if requested, but strictly speaking, I wasn't playing in the match any more, was I? They weren't too impressed with that argument and I had to lock up the car again and spend the next 90 minutes doing my best to pee into a bottle. After three or four gallons of water, orange juice, tea – anything that might force the issue and make me go – I finally provided the sample and away I went.

It wasn't the easiest of trips. I don't actually know how many service stations there are on the M1 between Leeds and London, but after downing all that liquid, I had to stop at just about every one of them and charge across the forecourt, into the gents, back to the car and away again.

When I finally arrived at the team hotel, there was a message on the phone in my room from Alec Stewart, the England captain. 'Good luck, all the best. You're here because you deserve to be here and because you're good enough to play for England. We're meeting in the bar at about seven o'clock if you want to come and have a drink. No obligations. You've played in plenty of big games and you know how to prepare. Might see you later.'

Being on début, I thought I'd better do the right thing and go down and say hello to the lads. I had a shower, changed and arrived at the bar five minutes early.

The only person there was Bob Cottam, the bowling coach. 'Congratulations, Oscar! Get yourself a drink, there's a tab on behind the bar. Have whatever you like.' I ordered a pint of lager and joined Bob at the table. One by one, the rest of the players came in. Same routine for them all. Walk over to the table: 'Well done, Oscar.' Walk over to the bar – and then order a mineral water, a fresh orange juice, a diet coke and so on. By the time we had all sat down, I was the only one with a pint. I remember thinking: 'Bloody hell, I've dropped a right bollock here.'

Nobody said a word, though. And with my reputation, it probably wasn't a great surprise to see me tucking into a pint on the eve of my international début. And why not? I'd had a pint the night before all my Lord's finals with Lancashire and not done too badly. So, on balance, there was no need to act any different because it was England and not Lancashire. Eight of us ended up going out for a Chinese and then back to the hotel for an early night.

Stewie had already pulled me to one side and told me I was 99 per cent certain to be playing and to get my head round the situation in the way I knew best. And when I rolled up at the ground the next morning, he gave me the nod. I was in.

I've often been asked if I was nervous. No, I wasn't. I went out with the attitude that I might never, ever play for England again. I was there as a replacement, not a first choice, and I was determined to take in every moment and enjoy myself. It was just like a one-day final with Lancashire, except this time I had the three lions of England on my chest. Proud? You bet. Overawed? Never. I wasn't a young kid, trying to make an impression. I was in my thirties, I'd been around and I knew everyone in the dressing-room anyway. I wasn't going to sit around in a corner wondering when to speak. Having Pete Martin in the side helped. We stood at mid-on or mid-off when the other was bowling and there was a fair bit of mickey-taking going on.

I bowled well enough, took a couple of wickets, including Aravinda De Silva, and we won the game by 36 runs. Then it was up to Edgbaston to play South Africa on the Monday. They made 244 for seven and we didn't bat well in reply. When it became obvious that we weren't going to win, we had to work out how many runs we would need to make it into the final on a faster run rate than the South Africans. We made it, and it was back to Lord's for the final two days later.

Sri Lanka again. And a bad mistake by the powers-that-be. They decided that the game would be played on the same pitch that we had used for the qualifying match against the Sri Lankans five days earlier. In that game, it was doing a bit for our seamers; but in the final it was worn, they played four spinners and hammered us. The spinners tied us down and we closed at 256 for eight Against their batting line-up, it never looked enough. As usual, they teed off early on, as they always do, and won it comfortably.

It was the end of the triangular tournament and, as far as I was concerned, probably the end of my England career. I'd played in all three games and I had done OK. But I didn't really expect it to go any further. I packed my bags and headed home.

When I arrived, the house was full of cards, telegrams, letters and newspaper cuttings. From family, friends, cricket lovers, cricket clubs. Even the Mayor of Rossendale and the Mayor of Hyndburn dropped me a line. They were all as proud as punch. The press described my call-up as a triumph for the journeyman pro and lots of the cards and letters took the same line. People seemed to think I had somehow fulfilled their dreams as well as my own.

I had a letter from across the Pennines, saying: 'Mr Austin, you are an inspiration to league cricketers everywhere. Those of us who are on the wrong side of 30, slightly overweight, bowl a nagging line and occasionally give the ball a bit of a biff, spend half our lives dreaming that one day Alec Stewart will be on the other end of the phone inviting us to make our England début at Lord's. Now it's happened to you – maybe it will be our turn next.' A less complimentary version of the same theme came from a pal in Lancashire: 'If a fat bastard like you can play for England, there's hope for all of us!'

With an Ashes tour coming up and a few one-day tournaments here and there, including a three-way series with Sri Lanka and the Aussies at the end of the Australian tour, it was 'watch this space' time until the squads were announced. It was no great surprise when I wasn't in the party for the Ashes tour. But after they decided to delay naming the squad for the one-dayers Down Under, I was named in the team to play in a one-day tournament in Bangladesh. It might not be everyone's dream tourist destination but I was thrilled to bits.

Even so, I worked out in advance that Bangladesh was unlikely to provide wickets that would be suitable to my type of bowling. And so it proved. They were flat, no grass, no pace, no bounce. We struggled to get the ball above stump height. We played South Africa in the first game and made 280. They knocked them off with no trouble at all and I remember thinking that if these were the kind of wickets I would be coming across in my international career, I wouldn't be around much longer. Wrong.

But a fair amount of water still had to flow under the bridge before my name appeared in the England squad for the 1999 World Cup. The first item on the agenda was a knee operation. The knee had been giving me problems towards the end of the season and I'd been told it would have to be 'cleaned out' over the winter. A sort of MOT job, I suppose. But I would have been ready to go through the pain barrier for another 12 months to stay in with a shout for the World Cup. I just needed to know where I stood. So in the end I phoned David Graveney, the Chairman of Selectors, and asked outright if I was going to be in the one-day squad for Australia, because if not, I could have the op there and then and still be available for selection. He said no, I wouldn't be going to Oz – but I still had every chance for the World Cup. So I went straight into hospital and had the op. I was up and about again before Christmas.

But would I be in the squad? The waiting seemed interminable. They named a party of nearly 40, whittled it down to 28, then 22 before choosing the final 15. Why the hell the rules don't allow countries to name their 15 straight off and put a few more on standby, I'll never know. In these situations, it's far more disappointing to come so close and then miss out at the end than to learn your fate early on. But I managed to hang in there until D Day finally arrived and turned up for training at Old Trafford, hoping against hope that I'd get the nod.

We were having an indoor net and I was standing at the back, waiting for a bowl, when Deborah Simpson, Lancashire's Media Relations Executive, called me over. 'Can I have a word, Ian?'

'Aye, of course. What's up?'

'Congratulations! You're in the World Cup squad. And there's a load of press outside wanting an interview. Can you spare them a few minutes?'

So that was it. I was in. And that's exactly how I found out. From a member of the Old Trafford staff. I never did receive an official letter telling me I would be a member of England's party for the 1999 World

Cup. I didn't even get a phone call from one of the five people on the selection committee. It wouldn't have been too much trouble, surely. There were only 15 players in the squad after all, 14 if you don't count Alec Stewart who had already been named captain. Surely they could have divided up the squad into five groups and given us all a personal call. It wasn't too much to ask – and I hear lessons have been learned. A good thing, too.

It was the same with the newspaper reports as they assessed the squad the next day. I was one of several players singled out as doubtful because of my knee operation. I would have to prove my fitness. But no one in any official capacity told me that or took the trouble to come and ask me how I was doing. There was just a constant flow of speculation about my knee, Michael Atherton's back, Neil Fairbrother's hamstring, Graham Thorpe's back. I read that I would have to undergo thorough preparation and tests. But no one took the time out to mention it to me before informing the press.

Lancashire was due to leave for a pre-season tour to South Africa before the World Cup squad assembled. And although me and Athers weren't originally on the tour, we received a message from Lord's, via Lancashire again, that we were to go out and get some cricket under our belts and then link up with the rest of the squad for the Coca Cola Cup in Sharjah a couple of weeks later. In the meantime, the rest of the players were due to play a few warm-up matches in Pakistan.

That was all right in theory, but after playing in a one-day game and the first day of a four-dayer, I came down with food poisoning and was confined to my room for the best part of a week. I proved my fitness on shuttle runs between bed and toilet . . . and in an organised fitness test at the Sports Institute in Cape Town.

So far, so good. But instead of me and Athers staying on in South Africa until it was time to move on to Sharjah, there was a change of plan. We were told to fly back home, link up with the rest of the squad and take part in the Pakistan series after all. Mike and I arrived back at Heathrow on a Friday morning and jetted out to Pakistan Saturday night. That little lot finished Athers' World Cup before it even began. You don't need to be a Harley Street back specialist to know that one of the worst things for dodgy backs is long-haul flying; you don't have to be a cricket anorak to know that Mike Atherton has suffered from long-term back problems. So it didn't come as a major surprise to me that Athers could hardly walk by the time we reached Pakistan. His back had seized up completely. He went to see the manager and physio and told them he wouldn't be able to play in the World Cup. He was booked on the first available flight out. More hours on a plane.

We were out practising when he left the team hotel. When I returned to my room, there was a note pushed under the door. From Athers. He wished me all the best. Told me I'd been picked because I was good enough to play in the World Cup and to go out and show people what I was capable of. Not to worry about the fitness – that's only two per cent of what this game is about. It's all in the head. I'd done it often enough for Lancashire, now go and do it for England. It was a tremendous gesture. He had every reason to be completely gutted. He'd worked his backside off in South Africa, playing, netting and putting in loads of extra fitness work. For it all to end that way must have been devastating for him. But he still found time to push a note under my door before he started the lonely trek home.

I was as sick about it all as he was. Why couldn't we have completed our preparations in South Africa and cut out the Pakistan leg before joining the squad for the Coca Cola Cup tournament in Sharjah, as originally planned? Why couldn't we just have flown direct from Cape Town to Pakistan? All that flying just didn't make sense.

Pakistan and Sharjah were pretty much as expected. The wickets were a million miles away from anything we were likely to encounter in a World Cup in England in May and June. We didn't play particularly well, and spent a lot of time chasing leather. But even so, there was a good feeling in the squad; we felt it was coming together and the spirit was building up well.

The idea was that when we returned to England, we would have some time off before the start of the competition. It made a lot of sense. I've always believed in the value of rest and after being away for two months or more, I wanted time with the family to recharge the batteries a bit. Not everyone feels the same way and ideally, the squad should have been given a choice: either take a break or play a bit of county cricket. Instead we had to link up with our counties.

For me, that meant spending a day watching the rain come down at Canterbury and four days doing damn all while it poured down at Lord's. We managed to get on the field for a National League game at Chelmsford which yielded 599 runs and more leather chasing, and then I sat out the Championship match at Leicester because I was a bit worried about a hamstring I'd tweaked while we were training in the rain. So in the end, I didn't get any cricket and I missed out on time with Alex and the kids.

I had to put all that behind me when we finally got together as a squad down at our headquarters in Canterbury. I checked in at reception, collected the room key, opened the door – and there it was, laid out in front me: my England World Cup uniform and all my playing kit. Everything was neatly set out and everywhere I looked, I could see the Three Lions. It's a moment I will never forget. A dream. One of the proudest moments of my life. The nightmare came a couple of hours later when I reported for a team meeting and was confronted by about 6,000 bats waiting to be signed by all the players!

That first night was like a family reunion and I'd made up my mind that whatever happened, I was going to give it everything in terms of cricket and just accept the inconvenient side-issues as they came along. There were plenty of those, with official receptions, meetings and so on. We even had to drive up to London for lunch at the House of Commons with a collection of MPs and other dignitaries. A good PR opportunity but inevitably a complete waste of time. Inevitably, after a load of lousy weather, our trip to the Commons coincided with a perfect day for cricket. Instead of putting in a full day's practice, we were stuck on a bus for four hours. With hindsight, was it really necessary for the whole squad to be there when they could have been practising outside?

We beat Kent in our first warm-up match. I bowled well and took wickets. Around this time, talk started that I might be taking the new ball when the competition got under way. I opened the attack in the next two warm-up games against Essex and against Hampshire, three days before our first game against Sri Lanka on May 14.

It was team meetings all the way in the countdown to that opening match and the day before the game, Stewie took me to one side: 'Look, Oscar, you'll be playing in the first game and it's more than likely you'll be opening the bowling. How do you feel about it?' I had no problem with that. 'If you and Mark Ealham can tie up one end, we can let Goughie and Alan Mullally blast away at the other. If you pick up a wicket or two, even better.' That was the game plan. And it worked a treat against Sri Lanka. To restrict the world champions to 204 all out from 48.4 overs was exactly what we had in mind and I was more than happy with my own figures of two for 25 from nine overs. Ealham did well, too, with two for 31 from ten. Stewart hit 88, Hick 73 and we cantered home by eight wickets. So far so good.

David Lloyd, the coach, came up to me after the game. 'Well done, Oscar. But were you a bit nervous?' he asked.

'No, not really, it went OK.'

'Right. I just thought you looked a bit edgy, that's all. A bit wary.' I couldn't work that one out. I certainly didn't think I'd bowled any different from any other big game, and my figures were good.

Next stop Canterbury. Opposition: Kenya. I opened the bowling again. I removed their opener, Otieno, straight away and Tikolo, the next man, got a huge nick three balls later. We all went up. Not out. He went on to give himself a bit of room and slapped it about for a while, finishing up with 71 out of their total of 203. Once again it was nowhere near enough, and this time we got home by nine wickets.

My figures of one for 41 didn't look as impressive as they had at Lord's but if that Tikolo decision had gone for me, who knows what I might have finished with? As it was, in two games, I'd taken three for 66 from 18.4 overs and we'd won them both by a distance. You couldn't ask for more than that and I was on a real high. We all were.

The crunch came against South Africa at The Oval four days later. There was another team meeting on the night before the match. Once again, Stewie pulled me to one side before the start.

'Can I have a word, Oscar?'

'Sure, what's the problem?'

'No problem. You're not playing tomorrow, that's all.'

I'm not often lost for words. But I had to make an exception in this case. I just couldn't take it in. I could only mumble: 'Why?'

'We're picking Angus Fraser instead. He's got a good track record against South Africa.'

I was beginning to get my voice. 'Fair enough. But how do I set about getting a good track record against these sides if I'm not even picked?'

'It's been a selection decision. Angus is playing and you're not.'

'Right, fine.'

It wasn't fine, of course. I was absolutely gutted. What had I done to deserve it? But I wasn't going to start rocking the boat – and, of course, I've never had anything personal against Gus. So I kept quiet. But I was bitterly disappointed.

The next morning, we finished the warm-up and I was strolling off the field after taking a look at the wicket. The teams had already been announced. Hansie Cronje, the South African captain, came over as I was walking off.

DREAM TEAM ONE: THAT'S ME, FRONT ROW, SECOND LEFT, WITH THE SCHOOL FOOTBALL TEAM. I LATER SIGNED SCHOOLBOY FORMS WITH BOLTON WANDERERS – AND THEN THE CRICKET BUG REALLY TOOK A GRIP.

DREAM TEAM TWO: HASLINGDEN UNDER-18S, LANCASHIRE LEAGUE CUPWINNERS IN 1983. I'M IN THE FRONT ROW, SECOND RIGHT. AND YES, I WAS A BIG LAD EVEN THEN!

DREAM TEAM THREE: THE LANCASHIRE FEDERATION UNDER-19 TEAM IN 1985.
I'M IN THE BACK ROW, FAR RIGHT. CAN YOU SPOT MIKE ATHERTON, WARREN
HEGG AND NICK SPEAK (AMONG OTHERS!)?

DREAM TEAM FOUR: CELEBRATING CLITHEROE'S VICTORY IN THE RIBBLESDALE LEAGUE
RAMSBOTTOM CUP IN 1986. I'M IN THE BACK ROW, FAR RIGHT, ONCE AGAIN.

DREAM TEAM FIVE: MY FIRST SPELL WITH MAROOCHYDORE CC, QUEENSLAND.
AND GUESS WHO IS IN THE BACK ROW, EXTREME RIGHT, YET AGAIN?

A LOAD OF BULL FOR BULLY. WELL, CRICKETERS HAVE TO DO *SOMETHING* IN THE WINTER – AND
HUMPING THESE CARCASSES AROUND WORKED WONDERS FOR MY THROWING ARM.
PICTURE COURTESY *LANCASHIRE EVENING TELEGRAPH*

CAP THAT! I RECEIVE MY LANCASHIRE COUNTY CAP FROM CYRIL WASHBROOK –
THE PERFECT HANGOVER CURE ON THE DAY AFTER OUR BENSON & HEDGES
FINAL WIN AT LORD'S IN 1990.

OLD TRAFFORD'S JOLLY BOYS' OUTING. WE TAKE OUR PRE-SEASON
TRAINING SERIOUSLY AT LANCASHIRE.

CHAMPAGNE MOMENT. CELEBRATING OUR 1996 BENSON & HEDGES
WIN WITH WARREN HEGG, GARY YATES AND MIKE WATKINSON.
PICTURE COURTESY PHILL HEYWOOD SPORTS PHOTOGRAPHY, BLACKPOOL

ANOTHER LORD'S VICTORY. THIS TIME IT'S THE 1998 NATWEST TROPHY
FINAL WITH WASIM IN CHARGE OF THE SILVERWARE.
PICTURE COURTESY ALAN SHEPHERD, BLACKPOOL

WELCOME ABOARD, JOHN. WITH MY BENEFIT CHAIRMAN
JOHN COTTON BEFORE THE OFFICIAL LAUNCH.
PICTURE COURTESY PAUL AGNEW PUBLIC RELATIONS, BLACKBURN

GAME FOR A
LAUGH . . . I'VE
JUST INFORMED
DIGGER MARTIN
THAT IT'S HIS
ROUND TONIGHT.
PICTURE COURTESY
D & J DAWSON,
SPORTS
PHOTOGRAPHY,
ROSSENDALE

ANOTHER DAY, ANOTHER CUP. THIS TIME IT'S THE 1999 CGU NATIONAL LEAGUE TROPHY. PICTURE COURTESY D & J DAWSON, SPORTS PHOTOGRAPHY, ROSSENDALE

THE A TEAM. AT HOME IN THE GARDEN WITH ALEX, VICTORIA AND MATTHEW. OSCAR, OUR JACK RUSSELL, WON'T BE FAR AWAY. PICTURE COURTESY D & J DAWSON, SPORTS PHOTOGRAPHY, ROSSENDALE

Now don't get the wrong idea – he wasn't looking for info for his bookmakers. Like I say, the teams had already been announced. And I'd known Hansie since we'd both played in the Super Sixes tournament in Hong Kong three years before.

'Why aren't you playing, Oscar? Are you injured or something?'

'No, I'm not injured. I don't know why I'm not playing. I've just been left out.'

'I'm not unhappy about that. We couldn't believe it when we saw you weren't in the side. We had you and Mark Ealham pencilled in as the two bowlers who would be hard work on this wicket.'

It was the end of my World Cup. We lost heavily to South Africa and from then on, I never looked like getting another chance in the games against Zimbabwe and India. The pitches at Trent Bridge and Edgbaston were always going to do a bit and I would have fancied my chances a lot. But I was left on the outside. We beat Zimbabwe, lost to India and when South Africa were beaten by Zimbabwe, we were eliminated from the second stage on run rate.

It was a desperate dressing-room afterwards. I remember seeing Neil Fairbrother just sitting in the shower with his head in his hands for about 20 minutes. We believed we were a good enough side in English conditions to get through to the second phase. But poor performances against South Africa and India and that 'odd' result between Zimbabwe and the South Africans cost us everything. But on the day, it's 11 against 11 – and our 11 didn't come up with the goods when it mattered.

It was a strange feeling for me. Yes, I was bitterly disappointed for myself and the rest of the boys that we hadn't gone through. But somehow I didn't quite feel part of it any more after missing those last three games. I'd been in the side that came out of the first couple of matches with a played two, won two record. And then I was sidelined. It was still hard to accept. I never had a problem with Alec personally, though. I've played against him for years and we've always got on very well. As far as I'm concerned, the message he left on my hotel-room answering machine when I was first called up says everything about the man and his thorough approach to the job.

Alec is a true professional. Totally organised. He's always immaculately dressed and is meticulous in his preparations for practice and matches. His kit is always 100 per cent and he has a place in his kit coffin for every item of equipment. I'm the same.

As a captain, Alec has always led from the front. He is totally committed, completely unselfish. He has always been ready to do anything if it's in the best interests of the team. If he believed for one minute that he was taking on mission impossible as captain, wicketkeeper and opening batsman, it never showed. Personally, I'm sure that was far too much to ask of anyone, even someone as committed as Alec. We're talking about three specialist roles and they all demand complete concentration. Three into one just doesn't go. And if you asked Alec to say, hand on heart, what his ideal role would be, I'm sure he'd go for captain and opening bat. He took on the wicketkeeper's job because it suited the balance of the side, but I'm certain it was number three in the pecking order.

During my time in the squad, though, he made me feel welcome and encouraged me to play a full part in team talks and so on. And he was one of those captains who allowed me to set my own fields. A definite plus. I remember, very early on he queried a couple of my field placings. But when I told him that's what I always did, he said it was fair enough by him. As a bowler, you can't ask for more. He made a point of coming over at the start of every over and talking about how things were going, making sure I was happy. He would make his suggestions, I would make mine and we'd come up with the answers. It was the same in the build-up to the World Cup and in the competition itself.

Alec was always open and fair. We spoke the same language. And while I found it hard to accept that I was no longer in the side, he did his best to keep me involved. It wasn't easy, because his priority obviously had to be the guys who were playing. But he seemed to know how I was feeling.

Looking back at the World Cup, the pluses far outweigh the minuses. I'd made up my mind to enjoy every minute and, as far as my own playing contribution was concerned, I did exactly that. In the end, things didn't work out as I had hoped, but above all, I can say I have represented my country in a World Cup. No one can ever take that away.

But our failure was a huge missed opportunity for English cricket. For the first time in years, we had a chance to put ourselves on the back pages of the tabloids on a regular basis, instead of stories about a footballer chipping his nail varnish in training or yet another transfer saga involving an overseas star. If we could have got through to the second phase, the semi-final and possibly even the final, we would have given the game a massive boost in this country, at international level, the county game and amateur cricket. All of a sudden, kids would have wanted to play cricket again instead of squinting at computer games. Sponsors would have been falling over themselves to get a slice of the action.

At least our failure provided the spark for a rethink about the way our international cricket is approached: ECB central contracts for starters. A good idea? For bowlers, yes, they're a great idea. Fast bowlers need rest. The last thing an England paceman wants is to finish a Test, drive five hours up the motorway, snatch a couple of hours' kip and then rock up for a county game the next day. He needs a pat on the back, a week's rest, a couple of net sessions and then get up and running again.

It's different for batters, though. If you're in nick, you don't want to be sitting on your backside doing nothing; you need to be out there scoring more runs. The bad times will come along soon enough. And if you're in a bad trot, you don't need a rest, you need nets and practice out in the middle. So it works both ways.

Central contracts are going to make life difficult for some of the counties. In the 2000 season, for instance, Yorkshire and Lancashire both had three players on contract while one or two Division One sides didn't have any. We can expect that pattern to continue in the future. So if we're going to go down the road of seven Tests and a triangular one-day series every summer, some counties will more or less have to write off their top performers for most of the season. Their teammates will just have to accept that and get on with job without the big names. That's the nature of the game. It's no good looking for excuses if things don't work out. Any young cricketer worth his salt should be saying: 'Right, this is my big opportunity. I'm going to make it impossible for them to leave me out when one of the England boys decides he needs a game.'

But none of the ideas that have been bandied about aimed at improving the standard are going to work overnight. There is a long, hard road ahead for English cricket. I happen to believe that man for man, most of the England players are as good as, for example, the South Africans who beat them in the 2000 series out there. What they don't have is the same level of confidence and self-belief that the Aussies and South Africans have been showing for years.

Graeme Hick is a classic example. Ever since I came into the first-class game, he's really filled his boots against Lancashire and every other county, for that matter. He's scored over 100 first-class hundreds, so he can't be a bad player, can he? And when you think that he's spent his entire career at Worcester, where the pitches are not always the best for batters, it makes you wonder how many he would have scored if he'd played on a true surface every week. Yet he has rarely showed the same qualities at Test level. Why? As Mike Atherton said to me before the World Cup, cricket is played in the mind. And that applies more and more the higher up the ladder you go. Some players can hack it; some can't. But the winners will only come through if they are certain that the people in charge really believe in them, too. It's so easy to have doubts in this game. Players have to be able to go out there and relax, play their own natural game, knowing that a couple of failures aren't going to mean the chop. And if England's coach Duncan Fletcher can give our top cricketers that kind of belief and self-confidence, we might discover that the players being produced at county level aren't quite as bad as everyone likes to make out. Beating the West Indies last summer was a start, but long-term success isn't going to happen overnight.

Two divisions in the County Championship will help. It's bound to introduce more competitive cricket right through the season. Let's be honest, there have been times in the past when sides have more or less packed it in around the beginning of August, knowing that they weren't going to win anything. And there was a lot of meaningless cricket around.

Like our game at Derby in 1995, the final fixture of the season. When the match began, we were safely installed in fourth place and couldn't move, either up or down. But we were also facing a fine for slow over rates during the season, which would have just about swallowed up most of our prize money for that fourth place. Ridiculous! So we decided to go hell for leather with the overs. Pete Martin and Glenn Chapple bowled about 25 overs in the first hour, the fielders raced to their positions between overs. It was the same in the second innings, with me and Digger setting the pace this time, and we finished up with an over rate of around 22 for the whole game. We avoided the fine. But I'd be the first to admit it was a farce, and we played some awful cricket in the process. Derby won the game at a canter. A total non-event.

That was an extreme example, but there have been a lot of meaningless games played towards the end of a season and I'm sure promotion and relegation will improve the situation. If you're in the bottom three with three games to go, you'll be fighting like hell to stay in the top division. No one will be settling for halfway house. Having said that, I'm not totally convinced about three up and three down when there are only nine sides in each league. It's like having eight teams promoted and relegated between division one and division two in football – too many. We'll have to see how it works out.

The same applies to player transfers. The current set-up where clubs can stop a player moving to another county will go by the board eventually, but I can't see a soccer-style system, where top players move just to stay in the top division. Yes, the so-called big clubs are going to want the best players on board – but are they going to sign Test cricketers who are on ECB contracts and might only be available for a handful of games? No. There's not much point signing Graeme Hick, Alex Stewart and Michael Vaughan to strengthen your batting line-up if they are going to spend the summer playing for England. You'd be back to square one.

We'll see what happens a few years down the road but overall, I refuse to accept that county cricket is a waste of time. Mike Atherton put the cat among the pigeons in a big way when he came back from last winter's South African tour and said that the county game serves no useful purpose as far as developing Test players is concerned. Sorry, Athers, but you're wrong there. County cricket didn't exactly give you a bad start, did it? And there have been plenty of overseas players who have seen it as the perfect stepping stone between their domestic game and Test cricket. Courtney Walsh is on his way to 500 Test wickets and he didn't just learn his trade in Jamaica. Playing county cricket for Gloucester hasn't done him too much harm, has it?

And there's a guy by the name of Viv Richards who learned what it's all about in the county game with Somerset and came back to haunt England in Tests. And there are plenty more where Courtney and Viv came from, top overseas players who have perfected their game in the County Championship.

That's what our top players should be doing, too. There has to be a direct route from league cricket into the county game, and on from there into the Test side. Anything else simply doesn't make sense.

I am prepared to accept that the county game isn't as strong as it was when I first started playing. And yes, of course there's a huge gap between Test and county cricket. But you could say the same about any international sport. There's no point just writing it off as a non-event and saying that it will never be a breeding ground for international players. Let's take a look at what's wrong, and work out how we can put it right.

I've already said that two divisions will make the game more competitive and eventually improve players' mental approaches. And then there's the question of pitches. It's as plain as the nose on your face that we aren't going to produce top-class players if we don't have decent pitches. In my 15 seasons, I've seen them all. We've had years when the batters have been able to go out and fill their boots on tracks that have given the bowlers no help at all. Like our game against Surrey at The Oval at the start of the 1990 season. I was the lucky one. I missed out on a place in the Lancashire side. The rest of the boys enjoyed the dubious privilege of performing on one of the flattest tracks in history and using a ball with virtually no seam. There was nothing at all for the bowlers: Surrey scored 707 for nine declared and we replied with 863 all out. Neil Fairbrother scored 366 and there were hundreds for Athers and Gehan Mendis and a double ton for Surrey's Ian Greig. The only interest in the game was whether we would make it into four figures.

We've also seen the other side of the coin, with pitches where a seamer can drop it on or around a length and come away with a five-for or a six-for because the pitch does the rest. Put that bowler in the Test arena and he disappears all round the ground.

There has to be consistency. We all know what a good pitch should be, and the ECB have established guidelines for pitch preparation. There should be pace and even bounce; something in it for both the bowlers and the batters if they have the technique and perform well. But how many of those do we see in a season? Not a lot. We must get rid of self-interest among the counties. We've all been guilty of it. Counties prepare pitches to suit their own bowlers and back themselves to get a result, hopefully without bringing the pitch inspectors rushing round. But is that in the long-term interest of English cricket? No.

The answer is in the hands of the authorities. They have appointed pitch inspectors, whose job it to go round the country and take a look at any dodgy tracks. They have the power to deduct eight points on the spot if the pitch is not up to scratch. And they should be using that power regularly. If four-day matches are ending in two days, there's usually something wrong somewhere. And if clubs are producing poor pitches to get a result, they should be punished. If the inspectors show their teeth and start lobbing a few eight-point penalties around, we might just see counties taking real action to improve their playing surfaces instead of just paying lip service to the rule book.

PART THREE

JUDGEMENT DAYS

9
THIS IS YOUR CAPTAIN CALLING...

Rightly or wrongly, Austin has never been seen as captaincy material. Yet his one spell in command brought non-stop success to a couple of sides on the other side of the world. In the process, Austin earned a host of plaudits from the local press for his 'inspirational leadership'.

The Oscar School of Captaincy has, so far anyway, only had one active season. But it was a hell of a successful one – 1991–92, my second spell with Maroochydore CC on the Gold Coast in Queensland. I landed in Brisbane on a Saturday morning after a 24-hour flight, to be greeted by Ron McMullin and one or two more club officials.

'Welcome back, Oscar. Good to see you, mate. The game starts in a couple of hours. And you're captain.'

'Oh aye? Right then.'

There wasn't a lot more I could say, was there? Talk about being thrown in at the deep end! The club had been reorganised in the four years I'd been away, and was now running a senior team and an Under-21 side. I was skipper of the big boys and given overall charge of coaching, nets and so on.

I was a bit apprehensive at first and needed a couple of games under my belt to get the feel of things. There were quite of a few of the lads I didn't even know. So I asked the committee to help with selection for the first fortnight. After that I was on my own. I enjoyed every minute.

We soon put together a fairly settled side, and as long as people were prepared to put in the effort, that was good enough for me. What more can you ask? If players try their best and it doesn't work out, so be it. There were some good decks around, so often it was a case of keeping it tight, keeping the pressure on, working for the opening – and then taking it. The boys responded tremendously.

From day one, I tried to be 100 per cent honest and open with people. It's easy to go into the dressing-room after nets, put your arm round a lad's shoulder and tell him he's been picked for the first team. You're always on a winner there. Sitting down with the player who's been dropped and explaining why he's been left out is another matter. I always gave them a reason why, and told them what they needed to do to regain a place in the side. Looking back, I like to think they respected me for my approach, but that was certainly the downside of the job. It always will be. But it has to be done honestly, openly and fairly – and not just at an amateur club in Queensland. The same applies at all levels, right through to the very top.

I've always believed that team spirit is absolutely crucial in the amateur game. Correction: at any level. If it isn't fun, why bother? And my first priority was to make sure there was a good atmosphere around the place. That's a pretty straightforward business with the Aussies, because they all turn up for nets anyway and enjoy a beer or two in the bar afterwards.

But while I'll have a good time with the best of 'em, I'm also a bit of a stickler for discipline. Straight away, I established a set of rules, with small fines for anyone who stepped out of line. We had a dress code, a time to turn up for nets, a time to report for matches and so on. Then there were fines for anyone who dropped a catch. If you missed one it was a couple of dollars, two catches dropped and it doubled and so on. And there were big problems if you took the easy option and didn't even go for the catch. There were fines for stupid run-outs, getting out to poor shots, no-balls, wides. And I ran a Wally of the Day Award and a Wasted Day Award.

There was a serious side to it, of course, because it kept everyone on their toes. But basically it was light-hearted stuff, and the fines weren't draconian by any means. And, as judge and jury, I was prepared to sit down and listen to appeals.

'Missed chance, what chance? I don't know what you're talking about, skipper. It never bloody carried in a million years.'

106 BULLY FOR YOU, OSCAR

'It did from where I was standing. Fine doubled on appeal!'

At the end of the season, the skipper/judge/jury/appeals court/treasurer totted up the kitty and we all got on a boat, sailed out to one of the islands and had a wonderful day on the beach. We also won the league and were beaten in the challenge final after I'd returned home. And, as I mentioned in an earlier chapter, I was asked to captain the Sunshine Coast team in the regional series and we won it for the first time. So perhaps the Oscar School of Captaincy has a bit going for it after all.

Lancashire have obviously never thought so. I've been on the scene for around 15 years now and as far as I know, my name has never been in the frame as skipper. I've played under Clive Lloyd, David Hughes, Neil Fairbrother, Mike Watkinson, Wasim Akram and now John Crawley and I'll be talking about them all in a moment. But the chance to run the show myself has never been on offer – or if it has, nobody has told me about it.

Would I have liked the job? Yes, of course I would. I reckon I know what the game's all about these days, and while the man management skills I learned Down Under might not be so easy to apply here, the basic principles are still the same. I believe I would be able to instil the right kind of spirit in a squad of 20-odd professionals.

I might not find some of the other duties a captain has to perform away from the dressing-room quite so easy. I'd be OK with the media, I've never had any problems there. I take journalists as I find them and if they play fair with me, no problem. But I have to admit that diplomacy has never been my strongest suit and I might not find it too easy in the committee-room and dealing with men in suits. I've never been much of a man for committees and meetings. If something needs doing, I do it; if something needs saying, I say it.

As I've progressed through the game, captaincy has appealed more and more. As I've mentioned before, I want to go back into the leagues when the time comes to call it a day with Lancashire. As captain. Why? Well, with all my experience, I could never just kick around as another member of a team. And if I were playing as a professional, I'd want to take charge out in the middle and that would only undermine the captain. If I'm not involved with Lancashire, I usually call in at a local league game over the weekend, watch a bit of cricket and have a beer and a chat with some old mates. And I had a game or two for Haslingden as a substitute pro during the 2000 season. So I know what I'm talking about when I say there's a lot I could contribute.

BULLY FOR YOU, OSCAR

Don't get me wrong, I'm not criticising the existing standards. I accept that the players are amateurs who are basically out there for a bit of fun. But there's so much they could learn about where to bowl to people, what fields to set, how to pick up runs against each bowler. And that's exactly what I could teach them as an ex-county player. I could point young players in the right direction, give older players something to think about – and, in my own way, help to improve standards in amateur cricket.

It's called putting something back into the game that has given me so much, and there is no way I will be following the lead of so many ex-pros by throwing the kit in the loft and walking away when I retire from the first-class game. You'll be seeing plenty of Oscar in years to come, believe me!

Captains come in all shapes and sizes. I suppose my first big influence was Bryan Knowles, captain of Haslingden when I broke through into their Lancashire League side. At the time, Bryan was the best amateur batsman in the league and he imposed himself on the game as a batter and as a captain. He did things his way, and earned players' respect because of his ability, rather than his man management skills.

I was happy to do as I was told because as a kid, you are more concerned with developing your own game than studying the finer arts of captaincy. You don't start trying to tell someone 20 years older than you how to run the show. This principle applied even more when I made my Lancashire début in that Sunday game against Derbyshire at Buxton in 1986. Clive Lloyd was our skipper, widely acknowledged as one of the best captains in the game, and there was no way an 18-year-old had any intention of telling Mr Lloyd how he wanted his field setting. It was more a case of 'I've moved third man a bit wider this time, Oscar.' 'OK, skipper. Fine.' Say nowt, do as you're told and bowl to whatever field the captain wants.

The first captain who started to really make me think about my game was David Hughes. As I said before, Yozzer was a huge influence, first of all in the Second XI and then later when he took over as first-team skipper and I was making my way into the side. He was the best captain I have ever played under. He never set a field and then told me to get on with it. He would always ask me what I thought about it first. And instead of telling me I ought to make a change, he would say: 'I don't know about you, Oscar, but I fancy we could do with a man in close for this fella. What do you reckon?' Usually, I hadn't reckoned anything at all. But once Yozzer had sown the seed of the idea, I was able to see what a bloody good plan it was. So I'd say: 'Aye, skipper. I was just thinking about that myself.' Neither of us was fooled. If it didn't work, he'd come back and ask what I thought the next move should be. Again, he knew exactly what he had in mind all along but he wanted me to feel part of the decision-making process. And all the time, he was providing an insight into different approaches to different players and above all, he was giving me a bit more confidence in my own ability to think for myself.

Yozzer knew who responded to a kick up the backside and which people needed an arm around the shoulder. Usually I was in the first category – but there were times when I'd be a bit down and he'd come across and say: 'Come on, Oscar, it's going OK. If you're struggling a bit, don't worry. Leave that to me. Just keep it going. Be positive.'

By and large, though, there weren't any major downers. Under David's captaincy I learned what my game is all about and started to understand the mechanics of my bowling. I came to appreciate that I'm never going to blast sides out, but my consistency and accuracy can put the opposition under pressure. If I tie an end up, frustrate people, pick up wickets here and there, I'm doing my job. It's worked for me at Championship level and above all in one-day cricket. And even though I've slipped down the order now, I like to think I can still make a significant contribution with the bat, either winning a game or saving one. Basically, the player you see when Ian Austin is out there in the middle was moulded in those early days under David Hughes. David was an example to us all and when he finally decided to retire at the end of the 1991 season, he was obviously going to be a tremendously hard act to follow. The writing was on the wall when he left himself out of the '91 Benson final against Worcestershire. Neil Fairbrother was already second-in-command and took over at Lord's. He was given the job full-time when Hughes bowed out.

Assuming Lancashire weren't going to give one of the senior players like Allott, Fowler or Mendis the job on a short-term basis, there were probably only two serious candidates, Neil and Michael Atherton. But Athers hadn't had the nickname of FEC (Future England Captain – or that's the polite version, anyway) since his days as skipper at Cambridge University for nothing. It was clearly only a matter of time before he succeeded Graham Gooch in the England set-up. As I understand it, Lancashire spoke to Athers about taking over from Yozzer, but he felt it wouldn't be fair to do the job part-time. Because Athers was almost certain to be fully involved with England, somebody else would have had to lead the side in about 50 per cent of our matches and take on all the other responsibilities of captaincy. That simply wouldn't have been fair on anyone.

I have never gone along with the idea that a captain can combine county duties, on and off the field, with playing Test cricket. The captain needs to be around the team to see how his players are performing day in, day out. He should be there in the dressing-room, taking control – not nipping off to play for England every couple of weeks and then trying to re-adjust to the county game. Captaincy isn't about hearsay and statistics. Looking at the figures, a batsman may not have made runs or a bowler may have given a few away. But that isn't necessarily the whole story. Players do make sacrifices for their side, even when they're in the middle of a bad trot, and the captain needs to be around to see that for himself, not judge his players on their statistics in black and white. Take that approach and all of a sudden people will start playing for themselves instead of the team, and then you're really on a slippery slope.

To some extent, the England problem applied to Harvey as well. Looking back, he will probably agree that the Lancashire job came around a few years too soon. Like Athers, he was in the frame for the England Test side and was trying to establish himself as a five-day performer rather than a one-day batsman who is still one of the best in the business nearly ten years down the road. Harvey never quite got it together at Test level, but he still played two matches during his first season in charge at Lancashire and was usually mentioned in despatches when squads were announced over the next couple of seasons. I think that in the end his efforts to stay part of the Test set-up combined with his England one-day career and the Lancashire captaincy all became too much. By the time he handed over to Mike Watkinson at the end of the 1993 season, he'd had enough. Eventually Winker fell into the same trap, although he lasted for four years and during his time in charge Lancashire won the Benson in '95 and achieved the Lord's double in '96.

Mike was the obvious candidate for the job when Harvey packed it in. He was 32 and capped back in '87. He'd seen it all and done it as well. Mike was a good all-round player in either Championship or one-day cricket, who could bat in the middle order and do a good job with the ball, either seam up or off-spin. Won a few Man of the Match awards in both major competitions. Popular. Knew the game backwards. And, at the time he took over, not really rated as a future England player, although he'd been talked about once or twice in the past.

It just shows how wrong you can be. In 1994, Winker had a super season. He scored 831 runs and took 59 wickets in the Championship and even though we didn't pull up any trees either in the four-day game or the big one-dayers, we finished fourth in the Sunday League. In the process, the name of Watkinson began to get a few mentions on the Test grapevine. He maintained his excellent form at the start of the 1995 season, and the England rumour factory went into overtime. Sure enough, after the West Indies had won the third Test, Winker got the nod to make his début at Old Trafford. He scored 37 and returned match figures of five for 92. England won and Winker was in the side for the rest of the series.

The winter tour to South Africa was a turning point for Winker. He only played in one Test and generally didn't see a lot of action. That meant spending a lot of time in the nets working on his bowling. I've always believed that too much netting can do more harm than good. In the end, it blows your mind. And I'm sure that when Winker returned from that tour, he'd practised himself out of his well-worn groove.

We won both one-day finals in '96, but the Lancashire job gradually started to get on top of him over the next couple of years. He desperately wanted to win back his England spot and at the same time play fair by Lancashire and the rest of the lads. If anything, he tried too hard – if there is such a thing. His form suffered and he became tense: it's impossible to perform at your best when you're not feeling relaxed.

I don't think Winker's concerns with his own game affected his captaincy, but I'm sure that he was never really happy with the need to distance himself from the rest of the team. It's a cross captains have to bear and when you've been an integral figure in the dressing-room for so long, it isn't easy. Contrary to his rather dour image, Mike has a marvellous sense of humour and is brilliant on the after-dinner circuit. He has always played a big part in the dressing-room banter; some of his wisecracks are legendary. But as captain, he had to stand apart sometimes. Mike never really came to terms with that. Neither did Harvey, for that matter. In the end, they were like men with the weight of the world on their shoulders and I'm sure they would admit now that relinquishing the captaincy was just about the best thing they ever did.

Did they jump or were they pushed? A good question. I think both Winker and Harvey saw the writing on the wall and decided it was time to go. There is a limited lifespan on captaincy, depending on how successful you are as a captain and a player. As far as Harvey and Winker were concerned, a change of captaincy was the best thing for everybody in the end. It certainly speaks volumes for them both that they were welcomed straight back into the dressing-room without any questions asked, and that they were happy to become just one of the lads again.

Wasim Akram had never been anything else. Captain of Pakistan (on and off), one of the world's leading all-rounders . . . but still just Waz. And he never changed during his year in charge in 1998. He'd had a trial run in 1995, captaining the side in one or two games late in the season when Winker was away topping the England averages against the West Indies in the last three Tests. Waz was brilliant. He led from the front and bowled himself into the ground. If there didn't seem to be any way we could achieve a breakthrough, Waz would take on the responsibility. He was never a man for long team talks; just a short chat before we went out, when he would tell us all to give it 100 per cent and enjoy it. That's how he played it.

It was no surprise, then, when he was offered the job full-time at the start of the 1998 season. Waz was a world-class player and an experienced international captain, and he'd always been hugely popular in the dressing-room. And as an overseas player, he was guaranteed not to be called up by England. A big bonus.

From my point of view, it was marvellous to have a captain who knew exactly how it felt to be a fast bowler. It's a hard life, you know. When you look around the county circuit, there aren't that many bowlers around as captains; not too many people who know what we're really going through. Waz was different, though. He knew what his bowlers were working at, knew how important it was for them to feel happy about their field settings. If you bowled a no-ball or a wide or if it just wasn't working out, he wouldn't stand, hands on hips, as if to say: 'What the bloody hell's going on?' He'd come over and remind you that the same thing had happened to him a million times before – and at Test match level. He'd tell you not to worry: 'You've bowled a no-ball. That gives you an extra ball at the end of the over to get him out.' Waz would tell the bowlers they had nothing to prove to him. 'I know you can do it. Now let's go out there and prove it.' That sort of thing works wonders for players' confidence, and there isn't a bowler in the world who doesn't run on that.

So I was disappointed when he left after just one season. It was all a bit of a mix-up, to put it mildly, with different versions of the story flying around all over the place during the winter. There was a rumour that Waz had told Lancashire he didn't want to carry on. Then he came out and claimed he had never said anything of the kind. He would have had to miss the start of the 1999 season anyway, because of the World Cup – but Lancashire still signed Muttiah Muralitharan, who was also playing in the World Cup, as their overseas player. So one way or another, it was a sad way to bring down the curtain on such a brilliant county career.

Waz's successor was John Crawley. Creeps arrived from the Ashes tour of Australia and stepped straight into the job with strong ideas about how he was going to do it: 'This is my way, and it's the right way.' I could see where he was coming from. He was new to the job and wanted to show he was the man in charge, to impose his ideas on the team. It was no problem for me that, at 27, John was part of the younger generation, the new breed, if you like. A different generation with different ideas and a whole new outlook on the game. That can be a good thing. But there's still no substitute for experience and knowing when to seek advice.

John is a stubborn character and his approach could easily have gone either way. Experienced cricketers, particularly bowlers, know how they want to approach their own game and the captain should be ready to consult them rather than insisting that they do it his way. But the players were patient and, for the most part, tried to help John settle into the job. We accepted that he was going to make mistakes and hoped he would learn from them. He did. Although he was young, John was wise enough to hold his hands up and say: 'Right, there were times when I got it wrong. I'm the captain and in the end, it's down to me. But if you feel there are ways we can do things better, I want to know.'

At first, John fell into the trap of just setting his fields and expecting the bowlers to get on with it. Once again, this is a classic example of a batsman captain not understanding what makes bowlers tick. It's no good expecting a bowler to throw seven or eight years' experience away and start on a whole new tack. But he changed. Now, we'll talk in the nets about how bowlers approach certain situations and how batters react. Both sides are learning from one another.

John has learned quickly. He has grown into the job. He is a far better captain now than when he first took over from Waz. And I believe he will go on to become an even better captain as the years go by. A possible England captain? He is certainly a good enough player and if he continues to mature as a leader, he is certainly going to be in the frame.

So what makes a good captain? People talk about the mystique of captaincy and down the years, there have been skippers who, one way or another, have been able to drag that little bit extra out of their players. It all comes back to man management and leadership. And you need the breaks. Successful captains tend to be lucky captains as well. They bring on a part-time bowler to break a partnership, the ball goes up in the air, a catch on the boundary; and it's a tactical masterstroke. If the part-timer goes for a lot of runs in no time at all, it isn't quite such a good idea.

When push comes to shove, having a few decent players around doesn't do any harm either, whether it's at at Test or county level. Take Clive Lloyd, for instance. He is widely acknowledged as one of the top captains the game has ever produced after his success with the West Indies side in the '70s and '80s. He had a tremendous record. But he didn't have much success in his years as Lancashire captain, when the county was going through one of its more barren spells. People reckon that if a Test side has three or four world-class performers they'll take a hell of a lot of beating, and the West Indies sides Clive led just happened to include about eight world-class players. At various stages of his captaincy, Clive could pick four fast bowlers from Andy Roberts, Michael Holding, Joel Garner, Colin Croft, Wayne Daniel, Malcolm Marshall, the young Courtney Walsh, Sylvester Clarke, Winston Davis and Tony Gray. Not bad! Any of them could have walked into any other side in the world. Batsmen? Gordon Greenidge, Desmond Haynes, Viv Richards, Lloyd himself. Wicketkeeper? Jeff Dujon. All world-class. The back-up players weren't bad, either. There were batsmen like Alvin Kallicharran, Richie Richardson, Larry Gomes and Gus Logie, not to mention all-rounder Roger Harper, probably the best fielder in the world at the time. Again, those players were good enough to play for any other team in the game, so it's hardly surprising that the Windies didn't do too badly with Clive at the helm.

More recently, we've seen Mark Taylor and Steve Waugh described as great Test captains. But once again, they've been in charge of easily the best side in the world, with a string of world-class players at their disposal. I'm not suggesting for a minute that Taylor and Waugh aren't good skippers – but are Australia the best side in the world because they have the best players or the best captain? Let's face it, if you'd taken Steve and Mark Waugh, Glenn McGrath and Shane Warne out of that side, handed them a British passport and plonked them into an England line-up, perhaps we wouldn't be quite so worried about the state of the English game.

10
SO WHO NEEDS A COACH?

In 1999, Lancashire played the second half of the season without a coach, following Dav Whatmore's departure to take charge of the Sri Lanka national squad. In his absence, the county became the first winners of the two-division National League and finished second in the County Championship. Questions were inevitably asked, tongue-in-cheek perhaps, about the role of county coaches.

It certainly came as a bit of a shock when we were told that Dav would be leaving. At that stage, the club obviously didn't have an immediate replacement lined up, so it was decided that the players would more or less run the show themselves until the end of the season.

We must have done something right. We finished second in the Championship and even though Yorkshire knocked us out of the NatWest in the quarter-finals, we went on to become the first winners of the two-division National League. So who needs a coach anyway?

We do! OK, we held things together for the second half of the '99 season and finished up doing well, but there's no real alternative to a full-time coach or team manager. The idea of a player-coach just doesn't hold water, for obvious reasons. How would he maintain his own form if he was spending his time working with other players? How would he cope if he was in a bad trot and ready for the chop? And you can't expect a captain to take on coaching responsibilities as well. You need a focal point, someone who is in overall command. Someone like Bobby Simpson.

The appointment of Simpson as Lancashire coach on a two-year contract at the start of the 2000 season gave the club and the players a tremendous opportunity to move forward. At 64 Bob is not the youngest in the world, but his record speaks for itself. He has played at the highest level, captained his country and took over as coach of the Australian side in the late '80s, when they were at just about the lowest ebb in their history. He rebuilt them from scratch and their current position as the best side in the world is down to him. Bob has also had experience of the English game as Leicester's coach and on top of all that, he knows what makes Lancashire cricket tick after his year with Accrington in the Lancashire League in 1969.

Lancashire must milk Simpson's vast experience and knowledge and turn it to their long-term advantage. Anything less would amount to criminal negligence. He first met up with us on our pre-season tour of South Africa, and it was obvious that those few weeks were going to be a learning process for him as well as the players. He took time out to get to know us and assess our individual strengths and weaknesses. And he quickly showed that he is a good judge of character as well as a good cricketer.

Bob knows all about the man management side of his job. He's approachable: if a player doesn't think he's getting a fair deal, Bob's door is always open; he will give you a straight answer to a straight question – he won't avoid an issue, he'll tackle it head on, and even if strong words are exchanged there are no hard feelings afterwards. From the start, he wasn't afraid to hand out bollockings if he didn't think we had performed up to scratch. Which is fair enough. But above all, he is open and honest. And you can't ask any more of a coach: if players can't take honest criticism, they shouldn't be playing professional cricket. The bottom line with Bob is that he has succeeded at the very top. And it is up to everyone at the club to take on board all that vast experience.

So the Simpson era has started. But if you talk about Lancashire coaches, one name will always come straight to mind: David Lloyd, or Bumble, as he will always be known inside and outside Old Trafford. Bumble is a Lancashire legend. He played for the county for 18 years from 1965 to 1983, five of them as captain, and returned in 1993 as coach alongside David Hughes, the manager. He took over as full-time coach the following year, before leaving to take the England coaching post in 1996. I've always said there is a Red Rose running right through Bumble's heart. He lives, eats and breathes cricket, especially Lancashire cricket. Coming in as our coach was his dream job and I'll never be convinced that he was totally happy about leaving, even though it meant taking charge of the England set-up. He never said as much, of course, and no one is ever going to turn down the chance to coach his country. But I'm sure that part of Bumble stayed behind at Old Trafford.

He was always 100 per cent Lancashire, the complete enthusiast. He'd be first on the ground in the morning and, as likely as not, last to leave at night. Coaching Lancashire wasn't just a job to Bumble, it was the ultimate labour of love, and woe betide anyone who didn't share his total commitment to the cause. I always did. So, thank goodness, did the rest of the boys. But even then, there were times when Bumble's brand of enthusiasm was a bit too much of a good thing – particularly in Sunday League games.

Bumble had been a member of the great Lancashire one-day side of the '70s, so he was entitled to offer his opinion about the way his successors were setting about the task 20 years later. It wasn't always favourable. For one reason or another, we usually seemed to find ourselves batting second, chasing a half-decent score and falling behind the run-rate. Bumble would be pacing around the dressing-room, yelling What's going on? What's he playing at? Why aren't they doing this? Why aren't they doing that? On and on and on. It never bothered me. In fact, I used to kill myself laughing about it. But Bumble's ranting was all you needed if you were the nervous type, waiting to go in to bat with a match there to be won or lost. So the boys started to take evasive action of their own.

There are two home dressing-rooms at Old Trafford, one for the first team and another for the seconds. And as Bumble turned up the volume, the lads who were due to bat later on would sidle off into the Second XI tent for a bit of peace. At first, David didn't notice. Then some of the people who had been in and out decided they fancied the quiet life, too, and they also made their excuses and left. It reached the point where one week, Bumble found himself ranting and raving about Lancashire's performance to an empty dressing-room.

He didn't see the funny side of it at first. He called everyone together and asked what we thought we were playing at. He was furious. 'What the bloody 'ell's going on? Why are you all clearing off into the other room when you've got this big dressing-room here? I'm your coach and you should be sitting in here watching the game with me,' he stormed. There was an awkward silence. Then one of the lads plucked up courage and said: 'Well, to be honest, David, it's you. Chill out a bit. Stop carrying on. You're the one who's upsetting everybody.'

Another awkward silence. 'Right, well if that's the case, I'll bugger off.'

For the next couple of weeks, Bumble took himself off into the old captain's room, shut the door and wouldn't come out or speak to anyone until the close of play. In the end, of course, we all had a laugh and a joke about it and Bumble took up his old station once again. It wasn't long before he was banging on again at full volume.

That's the thing about Bumble. He usually sees the funny side of things in the end, and his after-dinner speeches are laced with jokes at his own expense. Mind you, it took a while for him to see the funny side of a dressing-room prank down at Derby in 1995, that game when we belted through our overs to avoid a fine that would have gobbled up our fourth-place prize money.

As you will have gathered earlier, the game was very much an end-of-term affair as far as the boys were concerned, but Bumble wasn't having any of that. He insisted that we go through the full routine before, during and after the match, even though the result wouldn't have the slightest effect on our season. Not surprisingly, we didn't see it that way and David spent most of the three days boiling over about our approach to practice and to the game itself.

Most of the players rocked up for the day's play at about 10.30 a.m. and Wisden's reference to our performance as 'feeble' wasn't a million miles from the truth. I remember going out in the first innings, throwing the bat at everything and reaching 80 off 51 balls by the time last man Peter Martin joined me at the wicket. I was well on course for the fastest century of the season until Digger got himself out, standing in front of a straight one from Dominic Cork. I vowed revenge. And sure enough, in the second innings I was at the crease again when Pete came in. He got a thick edge off his first delivery and as the ball trundled down towards third man, set off for a single.

'No!' I called from the non-striker's end, leaning on my bat.

'What do you mean, no?' bellowed Digger.

'You threw away my fastest hundred of the season, so I'm not bloody running an inch for you this time.'

He just scrambled back in and next ball got a top edge over the keeper for four.

Needless to say, that kind of behaviour was not designed to soothe Bumble's frayed temper, and by the time the match finished with us on the wrong end of a 282-run defeat, he was seething. Too angry for words. As it happened, he had a speaking engagement in Gloucester that night and he started to unpack his best gear to get changed. Little did he know that earlier in the day, Mike Atherton had cut all the buttons off his shirt and snipped the bottoms out of his trouser pockets. The missing buttons went into one of his shirt pockets.

Bumble put his shirt on. No buttons. The lads were rolling around, almost in tears with laughter. 'You bastards! You stupid bloody idiots. How am I supposed to stand up and speak with no buttons on my bloody shirt?' We suggested that he try his shirt pocket. He located the buttons. 'Very funny, very bloody funny. So now I've got to go to my hotel and sew these things on before the dinner, have I? Thank you very much.' With that, he got into his trousers, put his shoes on, took the buttons out of his shirt pocket and put them into his trouser pocket for safe keeping. Next thing, they were rolling around the dressing-room floor. Bumble was straight down on his hands and knees, scrambling under the benches in his best suit, calling us every name under the sun. In the end he could only find about three of them. He suspected Athers all along, and departed for Gloucester warning him to expect a ton of manure on his doorstep before the winter was over.

As a budding National Hunt jockey, Bumble would have known all about manure, of course. Jockey? That's another of Lloyd's claims to fame. On April Fools' Day 2000, he featured in the sports pages of *The Daily Telegraph* sitting astride a racehorse, looking decidedly uncomfortable. The story underneath reported that Bumble was about to take a career swerve, to become a jockey and fulfil a lifetime's ambition, which had been conveniently kept under wraps. No one within a million miles of the Lancashire dressing-room was fooled for a second but apparently, loads of readers were taken in – not to mention other sections of the media, who tried to grab an interview with Accrington's answer to Richard Dunwoody.

In his other life as a cricket coach, Bumble had returned to the Lancashire set-up when Alan Ormrod left. They were completely different. I've mentioned before how much time I had for Alan and what a huge part he played in turning me from a young hopeful into a first-team player. He helped with my mental approach as well as my technique, and would always be ready to have a quiet word. He was team manager as well as coach, and would see that the little hassles which can make life difficult for the players were avoided. You need someone like that. High-profile coaches don't want to be involved in transport arrangements, hotel rooms, the players' kit and so on. But they are important. And if there is a foul-up, it inevitably means that the players are not concentrating properly on the thing that really matters: cricket.

Bumble was far more upfront than Alan, in every way. He wanted the players to have quality time in the nets and we would be in there early in the morning, working on our game rather than just preparing for the day's action. He did a brilliant job and I'm not convinced that he was 100 per cent happy about taking over as England's coach. It was definitely Lancashire's loss and even after he had left, he was a regular visitor to the Lancashire dressing-room.

The players loved him, at Lancashire and with England. Nothing had changed when I was selected for the England one-day squad in 1998. Bumble was there, still bubbling along. It hit him really hard when we were beaten. But he was always there the next day, picking the players up off the floor with his boundless enthusiasm. He was accused of going over the top by playing recordings of Churchill's wartime speeches and having 'Land of Hope and Glory' booming out in the England dressing-room. But it was just his way of trying to get the message across that playing for your country really did matter. I don't think it did any harm.

Bumble was never going to be low-profile, either with Lancashire or England. And inevitably, there were times when he opened his mouth and put his foot in it in a big way. Like his 'We flippin' murdered 'em' quote after the first Test against Zimbabwe in Bulawayo in 1996, an opinion that was not totally in line with the views of everyone else who had watched the action. The match was pretty low-key, but burst into life on the last day, when England chased 206 in the fourth innings and the scores finished level. Bumble was in a lather because he reckoned Zimbabwe had been a bit negative, to put it mildly, during England's run chase. He was fuming over Zimbabwe's tactics and the words just came spilling out.

But no one could ever question his enthusiasm, his commitment or, for that matter, his knowledge. If Bumble made a mistake as England's coach, it was his decision to surround himself with batting coaches, bowling coaches, wicket-keeping coaches, fitness specialists, dieticians, all sorts. And while I accept that there are times when even the best players need individual coaching, you can have too much of a good thing. Having so many other people around eventually undermined

Bumble's authority. Nobody was quite sure who was actually in charge of all the different departments. Was it Bumble? Or was it the specialist coach? At Lancashire, there was never any doubt. With England there was. And that uncertainty probably cost Bumble his job.

Since leaving the England scene, he has gone into print, writing his memoirs of his time as coach. I haven't read the book, so it wouldn't be fair for me to comment on the contents. But if, as I've been told, David has used it as an opportunity to take a pop at some of the England players during his time in charge, then I'm disappointed. I've always believed that if you have something to say, it should be said face-to-face and not written down with the benefit of hindsight. I always thought Bumble felt that way, too.

His departure at the start of the 1996 season meant that John Stanworth took over as acting head coach. John was never going to be as upfront as Bumble and was more of a team manager than a specialist coach. He was always there for advice, of course, but was happy to stay in the background and keep things ticking over. And how! Even though we were disappointing in the Championship, we pulled off a Lord's double. If Stanny had been a football manager, he would have been offered a new contract. Instead, he was pushed sideways and Dav Whatmore was named as our coach for 1997. It was a hell of a shock. The word was that Lancashire wanted a high-profile coach, and I suppose Stanny was never going to fit that image. But a lot of people inside and outside the club reckoned he had a raw deal.

Dav had carved out a big reputation for himself as a player and coach in Australia, and led Sri Lanka to the World Cup in 1996. But he'd never been involved with the English game and it took him the best part of a season to realise that what works Down Under or with a national squad doesn't necessarily work here.

That 1997 season was one of the worst I can remember. We finished eleventh in the Championship, went out of the NatWest in the second round and failed to qualify for the knockout stages of the Benson & Hedges. The only bright spot was third place in the Sunday League, but we finished up six points off the pace.

Why did we have such a poor year? We were completely knackered. It never dawned on Dav that players need rest time as well as training and practice. His idea of the perfect working week involved nets, fielding practice and a training session on a Monday, more nets and fielding on a Tuesday, nets and fielding before the start of a four-day game on the Wednesday, a 100-over Sunday game and then back in the nets on the Monday. We kept getting hammered. Dav's response was to tell us we weren't fit enough and to step up the training. By the end of the season, most of the lads were just about dead on their feet.

To his credit, Dav did take time out to talk to the players and find out their views. He also saw for himself how much time we spend on the road in the English game, how little time we have for rest and recuperation. And he got the message. The 1998 season was the first time Lancashire had given their players year-round contracts. I'll be talking about the benefits, or otherwise, of that system later on. But in that first season, we were able to get all our fitness work out of the way before most counties had really reported back. From then on, it was more a case of maintaining those fitness levels than slogging it out day after day as we had done the year before.

The result was that we won the Benson & Hedges and the Sunday League and finished second in the Championship. It was one of our best seasons for years, and it was the first time in my Lancashire career that I was actually sorry to see the season end. Normally, by the middle of September every player in the land has just about had enough. County cricket is a long, hard slog and when the season grinds to a halt, we're all ready to put our feet up for a few weeks. But I can honestly say that in 1998, I could have gone on for another couple of weeks, no problem. It was a massive change from 12 months earlier.

Was Dav the victim of player power in '97? Not really, no. I prefer to think that he was a good enough man manager to talk to his players, listen to what they had to say and realise he had got it wrong. He came back for the 1998 season prepared to learn from his mistakes and his reward was two major trophies in the Old Trafford cabinet.

11

THE GREAT AND THE GOOD

Since joining the Lancashire staff in 1986, Austin has emerged as the latest in a long line of Red Rose folk heroes which dates back to the golden days of Roses combat and beyond. Yet in his time, the man from Haslingden has played alongside a few Lancashire legends, too.

When I set up Ian Austin Personal Security Services, I'll already have the name of one VIP on my books: Mike Atherton. It's a standing joke in the Lancashire dressing-room that I'm Athers' minder. It all started a few years back, when the boys had one of our winter nights out. There has always been a good social side to the Lancashire team, and we stick together out of season with golf days, nights out and so on. We don't pack our bags at the end of the season and say cheerio, see you next year. We enjoy one another's company and that's been one of the secrets of our success. We never make a fuss about it, and we don't expect anyone to pay much attention to a group of Lancashire cricketers out having a good time. We keep ourselves to ourselves and we know how to behave. Athers is just part of the gang.

Which is how it was when we all arranged to have a few beers in a club in Manchester a few years back. It was all pretty low key until one of the punters recognised Athers and decided he wanted to shake his hand and ask for his autograph. Fair enough, that's part of the job. Up to a point. The problem was, the fan went back to his mates and told them who was at the bar. Word soon got around that Michael Atherton was signing autographs.

Before long there was a crowd of about 30 people crowding round, wanting Athers to sign on the dotted line and talk cricket. Mike put up with it all for a while but I could see he was getting fed up, so I stepped in.

'Right lads, I think that's about enough, don't you? He's just popped out for a few beers with his mates, so can you back off now?'

I can't have got the message across. 'And who the hell are you?' I was asked.

'I'm his minder. And if you lot don't piss off, I'll shift the bloody lot of you.' It worked. The crowd dispersed instantly, the rest of the evening passed without incident and I've been down as Athers' minder ever since.

We go back a long way, as far as the Lancashire Federation Under-19 side at the 1984 Cambridge Festival that I mentioned in an earlier chapter. Mike has never really changed on or off the field. He's a bit bigger now than he was in those days . . . but not a lot. And he's even harder to get out, as the world's greatest fast bowlers have discovered to their cost over the last ten years or so.

We were playing a few one-dayers down at Cambridge so having a 16-year-old in the side who was struggling to get the ball off the square wasn't necessarily a prize asset. But he could play. Athers was the latest edition from Manchester Grammar School. And down the years, his game hasn't changed a lot. The technique is sound, but he doesn't look to dominate the bowling. He'll occupy the crease, accumulate his runs and bat, bat, bat. And he likes nothing better than a good scrap.

Athers was a quiet lad then – but I suppose you would be when the rest of the team are a couple of years older than you. Even now, he's happy to stay in the background. He has a good sense of humour and is always ready for a spot of banter or a practical joke, but is never one of the ringleaders. He is not the world's tidiest cricketer, either. His corner of the dressing-room is a complete tip.

Athers is not the type of person who'll strike up a conversation with a complete stranger, and he's been stitched up often enough to be very wary of people he doesn't know. You won't often catch him off guard outside the dressing-room. But when he's sure of the company he's in, Athers will relax and have a laugh.

He likes a bet and you'll often find him studying the form before embarking on his morning net. But money has never been a driving force; he doesn't give a damn about it. And fashion? Forget it! If it's comfy and it fits, that's good enough for Athers. He's been wearing the same pair of shoes for as long as I can remember: a pair of brown loafers. He admits that he's had them since he was at Cambridge University, and they're the most horrendous pair of shoes you could ever imagine. Battered to death. But Athers won't wear anything else and he swears he won't be throwing them out until they fall to pieces.

Needless to say, a few of the lads had other ideas a couple of seasons ago and a plot was hatched to burn the bloody things on the pavilion balcony after the final game. It was all top secret stuff. But somehow Mike must have got wind of the scheme, because the loafers never saw the light of day in that final match. But they were back in business the following March! No doubt, one of the reasons he's put up with them for so long is that he doesn't have a sense of smell.

Ather's poor sense of smell probably explains how Peter Martin's boots got overcooked when they came to be in Athers' oven. Digger used to stay with Mike when he first came into the Lancashire squad, and one day he'd been running around on a damp outfield all day and his boots were absolutely sodden. Pete decided to take them back to the flat and dry them out, and between them they came up with the idea of lobbing them in the oven. They switched it on, went back into the lounge and forgot all about the boots – until Digger saw the smoke. They dashed into the kitchen, rescued the burning boots and plunged them into a bucket of water. The soles of the boots had melted onto the floor of the oven, and there was smoke everywhere. In the end, they chucked the boots out on to the balcony and rumour has it that the burned-out hulks were still there two years later. Athers strikes again.

Just like he did when his mum came round to clean up and sort the mail a couple of weeks after Mike had set out on an England tour. The place was in its usual shambles, but this time there was also an evil smell creeping out of the kitchen. No, not Digger Martin's boots this time, but the remains of a plate of cheese and biscuits Mike had started but not finished eating before setting off. It had never crossed his mind to dump them in the bin, and all that was left was a huge pile of mould in the sink.

Possessions don't mean anything to him, either. A few years back we were both down to attend a charity function in Manchester, so Athers said I could sleep in the spare room at his flat. There was a big box in the corner. I took a peep inside. It was full of medals, awards, mementoes of some of the high spots of his career for Lancashire and England. They looked as if they'd been stuck in that corner of his spare room for years.

BULLY FOR YOU, OSCAR

He's the same with his England gear. At the end of a tour, he'll pack the essentials in his bag – boots, helmet, bats. The rest stays behind.

Athers was always set-up as an England captain of the future, and for a while it was a standing joke with the rest of the boys. Manchester Grammar, Cambridge, Lancashire, England: he was pencilled in as the golden boy of English cricket from an early age. Of course, there have been a few of those before and since who haven't made it, but there was never much doubt about Mike. He was always going to the top. But he never made a fuss about it and when the stick was flying, he joined in the fun and then went out and got on with what he did best – playing cricket. Mike has a tremendous cricket brain. Reads the game brilliantly. But even though he has captained England so many times, he never imposes himself in the Lancashire side. I've never known him to go up to whoever is captain and suggest what should be done. He waits to be asked.

And he didn't change one bit when he was appointed England captain, or when he lost the job. He knew it would happen one day. In fact, I think he prepared himself for it. He always said the job had a lifespan and he would know when it was time to go. He took over when we were struggling and set himself a period of time to turn things round. He knew what he wanted, but there were times when he was frustrated by the lack of progress. As a grit and determination player, he expected people to follow his example and wasn't a man who would give a rousing team talk. That just wasn't his style. The combination of David Lloyd and Mike would have been ideal – Bumble the cheerleader and Athers, the strong silent type.

In the end, the job started to get to him, again probably due to frustration. He knew the way forward, but things weren't moving quickly enough. And I don't think Athers could come to terms with the fact that not everyone had the same levels of application. That's when the Captain Grumpy image started. As skipper, you have to accept that you will be doing interviews, sometimes straight after the game. It's a part of the job. But it can't be easy when you have bad day after bad day, or if you personally perform but the rest of the side doesn't. Let's face it, things reached the stage where if the opposition got rid of Athers early doors, England would fold up. He had to carry that burden as well as the captaincy, so inevitably there were times when he wasn't exactly a ray of sunshine at press conferences. I could understand his predicament, and I'm sure he did the right thing when he quit after the West Indies tour in 1998.

But Mike is still our top player, the man the opposition are gunning for. And that's a situation he loves. There's no reason why he shouldn't be around the England scene for a while yet, even though we've said farewell to Captain Grumpy.

The Lancashire lads had a chance to enjoy the Captain Happy side of his nature when we played Yorkshire in a pre-season one-day friendly – if that term can ever be used to describe a Roses match – at Old Trafford a few years ago. He'd been to a charity do at a Manchester hotel the night before, a black tie dinner. Athers was on the top table with Ian Botham and Ian Woosnam, never the most reluctant pairing when it comes to having a good night out. Once the official side of the event was over, Beefy decided to have a bit of a bash with the survivors and started drinking them under the table one by one, before carting them off to bed and returning for more of the same. By all accounts, Athers hung in well and the first light of dawn was breaking over the Manchester rooftops by the time Beefy finally saw him off.

Fast forward a few hours, and there was a bit of concern at Old Trafford when he wasn't around by the time we had all reported for the warm-up at around 9.30 a.m. You could usually bank on Mike having his pads on by 9.45 at the latest, and starting to grumble because no one was ready to have a bowl at him. So when it passed 10 a.m. and there was still no sign of the skipper, questions started to be asked.

'Where the bloody 'ell is he?'

'I don't know. Wasn't he going to some charity do with Beefy last night?'

'Oh aye, that's it. He'll be along in a minute then.'

He wasn't. The clock moved on to 10.25, five minutes before the toss. David Byas, the Yorkshire skipper, ambled over and singled me out as the man most likely to know where our skipper might be.

'Where's Athers, then, Bully? It's time for the toss.'

'Don't know, David. I'll see what I can do.'

I nipped back into the home dressing-room, hoping that Mike had slipped in while I was talking to Bingo. He hadn't. We were just deciding who would take over and toss up when Athers appeared. He had arrived in a taxi, and was still wearing his dress shirt and dinner-suit trousers, with no tie, no jacket and no socks. They were no doubt back in the hotel room. And he was clearly still well pissed.

He dug into his kit coffin, put on the first bit of gear he could find, linked up with Byas and the pair strode out to the middle. At least, Byas strode out to the middle. Our captain took a rather less direct course as he wove his way out towards the wicket. They tossed up and Byas marched back, with Athers staggering along beside him with a silly grin on his face. The lads were killing themselves and so were the Yorkshire players.

Athers eventually made it into the dressing-room and sat down. 'Come on then, Athers, what are we doing? You've just tossed up. Are we batting or fielding?' I asked.

'I don't know. I can't remember.'

That was a new one on me. Our twelfth man was sent down to the Yorkshire dressing-room to find out what was happening. Word came back that Bingo had won the toss and decided to have a bat. So Athers led the Red Rose army into battle, and for the first hour or so it was definitely a case of captaincy by committee. Before he sobered up, though, Mike took an absolutely blinding catch at backward point – then just stood there laughing and looking at the ball in his hand as if to say, 'How the hell did that get there?' He was full of apologies afterwards. But none of the lads had any problems. He wasn't the first person to fall among thieves in the presence of I.T. Botham – and he won't be the last.

Wasim Akram was already one of the world's leading all-rounders when he walked into the Lancashire dressing-room to link up with the lads at the start of the 1988 season, the first of his nine years as our overseas player. But he fitted in straight away. He had to.

Waz had been playing in the World Cup that winter and signed on the dotted line at the end of the competition. He arrived after the start of our season because he was involved in Pakistan's series in the West Indies. One or two of the Lancashire dignitaries met him at the airport and brought him to Old Trafford. After a few minutes to say hello to the players and be shown his locker, he was hustled away to have lunch with the powers-that-be. We were due to leave on the coach that afternoon for our game against Notts down at Trent Bridge the next day, and Waz had brought his kit along with him and left it in the home dressing-room.

As it happened, there was some building work going on round the back of the pavilion and as soon as Waz's back was turned, two or three of the lads nipped out to the building site and collected a few bricks. We opened his bag, chucked the bricks in the bottom and then put all his new Lancashire gear on top. Waz returned from his lunch date, collected his bag and then struggled out to the waiting coach. As the new boy, he obviously didn't like to say anything at that stage about the weight of his bag.

In the dressing-room at Trent Bridge, there's a big table where we all leave our kit coffins as soon as we arrive. We open the lids and then tape them together so they don't keep falling down. We made sure a few of us got in first and left a space in the middle of the table for Waz, who had a hell of a job lifting his coffin up onto it. But as no one seemed to be taking the slightest interest in what was going on or offering to lend him a hand, he kept quiet. But he looked a bit baffled about it all.

When Waz opened up his case, all his new Lancashire kit was sitting proudly on top. He put on a T-shirt under his cricket shirt, then, after looking out at the weather, decided that his Lancashire tracksuit might not be a bad idea early-season at Trent Bridge. He was rooting around in the bottom of the coffin when he came across the first brick. Then another . . . and another. All his teammates just happened to have discovered that it was time to fasten their bootlaces, leaving a bemused Waz muttering to himself: 'What the hell is happening?' The answer was a ring of faces all helpless with laughter. Waz saw the funny side of it too, and uttered his first serious condemnation of his new teammates: 'You set of Lancashire bastards!' He's been one of the boys ever since.

Waz is the best all-round cricketer I have ever played with. On his day he was devastating, and his presence gave us massive confidence. Some of the innings he played were awesome. He didn't make many huge scores, but he could go in and turn a game around in the space of 20 minutes – like that first Lord's final when he battered the Worcester attack and lifted the whole team just when it looked as if we might be struggling.

Waz could conjure up brilliant bowling performances from nowhere on a day when it seemed as if we'd never get a wicket. He just blasted the tail away, time after time after time. Like a lot of sides, we have often struggled to get rid of stubborn tailenders, but not with Waz around. Nine, ten and jack never had a chance. As soon as we had seven or eight down, we knew we'd be putting our feet up back in the tent in a few minutes. Yorker, yorker, yorker. Then if that didn't do the trick, a high-speed bouncer and a dong on the helmet. Next ball, another yorker. Thanks very much. So simple in theory, but you need a special talent to produce it week in, week out. He was a tremendous performer.

But it wasn't just his cricketing ability that made Waz so special. He was also absolutely brilliant in the dressing-room. He settled in from day

BULLY FOR YOU, OSCAR

one and never wanted to be anything more than just one of the lads. He wasn't our overseas star; he was one of us. He took a load of stick from the other players, but was always ready to give it back with interest. And with Waz around, there was never any shortage of perks.

As soon as he arrived, he became the focal point for Manchester's Asian business community, who welcomed him with all sorts of gear: clothing, sports equipment, the lot. We'd all sit looking at these boxes, which seemed to arrive on a daily basis, and eventually Waz would get around to opening them, or asking one of the lads to open it for him. He'd take a look at what was inside and then tell the other players to help themselves. He gave the rest away to anyone who happened to be around or arranged for it to go to a good cause. He was incredibly generous.

One day, this huge box was delivered. It was full of footballs. Footballs for Waz? You must be joking! He was easily the worst footballer ever to grace the Lancashire dressing-room. Absolutely hopeless – and despite what he may tell you, he didn't improve much as the years went by. He spent all his time falling over instead of kicking the ball, and never managed to perfect the art of standing on one leg and booting the ball with the other without falling flat on his back. It was hilarious.

As well as clothing and sports gear, Waz used to be singled out for food parcels from local Asian restaurants wherever we played. We'd return to the dressing-room after a morning in the field to be confronted by naan bread, chapattis, cartons of kebabs, curries and so on. Loads of the stuff. All for Waz. He'd tell the lads to help themselves and we'd dig in.

On the circuit, Waz would always find time during an away trip to take us out to one of the local Asian restaurants. He was treated like a prince from the minute we walked in. He would ask the waiter to fetch enough food for the whole group and for the next hour or so, plate after plate would arrive on the table, all top-class stuff and far more than we could possibly eat. There might be six or seven of us round the table and enough food for 15.

Yes, Waz is a genuine Lancashire cricketing legend. One of the all-time greats. And his successor would surely have gone on to achieve the same status if only he'd had the time: Muttiah Muralitharan, a magical little man, on and off the field.

He was the happiest bloke you could ever wish to meet. Watch him on the box and he's always there with a big smile on his face; well, what you see is what you get. He loves life, he loves cricket. I don't think he ever really stopped smiling during the whole of his time at Old Trafford.

Nothing was too much trouble. Just after he arrived at Old Trafford, following Sri Lanka's exit from the 1999 World Cup, we had a photo-call for one of our new sponsors, a German lager company. One of us would have to put on the full Bavarian outfit, complete with lederhosen and a silly hat. We looked at Murali. A big smile. On went the gear and he was still laughing as me, Harvey and Freddy Flintoff sprayed him with lager for the publicity shots. Unlike the rest of us, he wasn't bothered about drinking the sponsors' product, either! He would sometimes have a brandy or a whisky and coke (loads of coke) in the bar at night, but by and large he was too busy talking cricket to bother about strong drink.

Murali was our Walking *Wisden*. I've never known anyone who knew so much about cricket – or anyone who could talk about the game for so long. There's a hell of a lot of international cricket being played all year round these days, but Murali knew about it all. Who was playing who, who had beaten who, who had scored runs and who'd taken wickets. He knew more about Lancashire's record than the Lancashire players themselves. We'd be sitting in the dressing-room or in the bar in the evening at an away game and he'd suddenly start talking about one of our games from years back. He'd know all the facts and figures and couldn't believe that the rest of us didn't remember every last dot and comma of the game he was talking about.

Once he got hold of the ball, it was virtually impossible to get it off him again. He was more than happy to bowl all day and let the quicks operate in rotation at the other end, and always with a smile on his face. And Murali's idea of a dream day was a chance to enforce the follow-on. Now, it has to be said that there can be times when enforcing the follow-on is a mixed blessing, to put it mildly. You slog your way through 100 overs or more, bowl the opposition out and then, instead of a shower and a rest, you have to start all over again. That's what happened when we played Glamorgan at Blackpool midway through the 1999 season.

It was a flat track and we went out and racked up 556 for six declared, with Athers notching an unbeaten 268. Then we bowled the Taffs out for 282. Murali bowled 48 overs and took six for 106. I bowled 19 overs, Richard Green bowled eight and Mike Smethurst five. Between us, the three pacemen were still 16 short of Murali's total. Even so, it was a hot day and we didn't fancy a re-run when John Crawley decided to put them straight back in. Murali? He was delighted. 'Just give me the ball,' he beamed. Then he went out and bowled another 40.3 overs on the run, taking four for 72 this time, and he loved every minute of it.

That game summed up Murali's approach to bowling and his overseas role at Lancashire. He was determined to be involved at all times. His first Championship game down at Gloucester was washed out before he had a chance to bowl. But in the next six games, he bowled 386.2 overs and took 66 wickets at just over 11 runs apiece.

I'll never know how he managed to keep going. But the ice pack played its part. Wherever Murali went, so did the ice pack. It was like a big rubber bag which fitted round his bowling shoulder. He'd come off the field at lunch after one of his marathon stints, go to the fridge, fill the ice pack, put it on his shoulder and sit there with a big grin on his face. Then as we got ready to go out again, he'd be on at the captain: 'Skip, skip, I bowl. Let me bowl.' He'd put in another 30 overs between lunch and tea, before heading for the ice pack once again.

But he was just as effective in the one-day game. Batsmen simply couldn't get him away. His only problem came when we played Warwickshire at Edgbaston. We arrived, had a look at the wicket and couldn't believe our eyes. It was a dustbowl. Murali was going to have a field day. However, it didn't quite work out that way. OK, he bowled his nine overs for 13 runs and took one wicket. But unbelievably for Murali, some of the runs conceded were wides. We couldn't believe what we were seeing when Barrie Leadbeater, the umpire, signalled a wide in Murali's first over. Wide? From Murali? Never! At the end of the over, he came over to me: 'Struggling, Bully. I just can't bowl on this.'

'What do you mean, you can't bowl? It's turning square. I could turn it on this bloody thing.'

'Yes, but pitch not wide enough.'

Murali was turning it so much that even if he pitched the ball on the very edge of the cut strip, it was still flying down the leg side. He solved the problem by bowling round the wicket; it was the only way he could pitch it on the wicket and keep it there.

Playing against Murali in the nets was an education in world-class spin bowling. Fascinating. Needless to say, a few of the lads decided they had worked him out and tried to give him the charge: 'Let's see what this guy's like when someone really gets after him!' – you know the kind of thing. Well, we soon found out. He'd turn the first ball one way, the next ball the other way and by the time the batsman had ended up halfway down the track trying to hit the third over the top, the message had got through. And every time a batter found himself stranded in no-man's land, Murali's smile would light up even brighter. What a lovely man!

He was two bowlers in one. He was so accurate that he did a containing job, and he was firing batsmen out all the time as well. Like I say, it was a dream for the pace bowlers because we could all stay fresh while Murali tied an end up.

Yet how he managed to stay so happy while the furore over his action continued to rage, I'll never know. From the start of his career, he had been forced to endure whispers that he was a chucker. But he was born with a slightly deformed right arm and always insisted that this made his action look a bit odd. The Sri Lanka authorities backed him to the hilt. But everything came to a head when he was called seven times for throwing by Australian umpire Darrell Hair in the Boxing Day Test at Melbourne in 1995. Soon afterwards he was called again, this time by Ross Emerson, in a one-day international. The International Cricket Conference stepped in and after filming Murali's action from 27 different angles and taking all sorts of medical evidence, he was cleared. Emerson called him again in 1999 but this time there was no follow-up and Murali arrived at Old Trafford with the slate officially wiped clean but the whispering campaign still going on.

Apparently there were times during the ICC investigation when he felt like just packing it all in. But he came through it and, like the other Lancashire players, he shrugged the whole thing off. He knew he was innocent and a string of medical tests and video evidence had cleared him of charges that at one stage had threatened to end his career and wreck his life. So why worry? That was his philosophy.

We'd all love to see him back. And hopefully he'll be able to find time to play in England again despite Sri Lanka's international commitments – they seem to be playing all year round at the moment. And now that Bangladesh have been granted international status, there is bound to be all sorts of tournaments between the two of them. But he'll stay in touch, that's for sure. He regularly telephones the Lancashire dressing-room to see how we're doing. A great guy.

Of course, the bottom line as far as the overseas man is concerned is producing the goods out in the middle. Murali and Waz certainly did that and they played their full part in the dressing-room, too. But even if you're the greatest bloke on the planet, life as an overseas player can be pretty tough if you're not scoring runs or taking wickets. As Steve Elworthy discovered in 1996.

We were looking for someone for one season only while Waz was touring over here with Pakistan. Neil Fairbrother had been in South Africa in the winter and came up with a couple of names: Elworthy and Steven Jack. Both were a bit sharp, apparently. Jack got the nod at first but had to withdraw because of injury, so the call went out for Elworthy, who had played for Rishton in the Lancashire League four years earlier.

He should have learned from the experience. But he came over and started dropping it on the length he would have used in South Africa – not a good idea on early-season English wickets, and he was slapped around a bit. As a batsman, he had the reputation of being a bit of a dasher and he was tried up the order as a pinch hitter. But again, that didn't really work out either. Elworthy was under pressure because he was following Waz anyway and inevitably, his confidence suffered. He found himself on the crest of a slump.

It reached a point where we eventually had to think about leaving Elworthy out of the side. He stayed in the line-up for the Championship, in the hope that things would turn around a bit. But as far as the one-dayers were concerned, he kept finding himself on the sidelines. Leaving out your overseas man is a big step and understandably he wasn't happy about it. But we'd done well without him and it was something he had to live with.

In fairness to Steve, he never sulked. He was always good value in the dressing-room. His chance to get back on track came when he was recalled for the Benson quarter-final against Gloucester and responded with four for 14 from ten overs. He stayed in the side for the semi against Yorkshire, taking one for 52 this time. But it was 50–50 between him and the off-spin of Gary Yates in the final and on the morning of the match, Gary got the nod.

Steve was devastated. His wife was over here already and his parents had flown in from South Africa to see him play in a Lord's final. To his credit, he didn't rant and rave. Instead he went walkabout, sat in his hotel room for a while and then came back to the ground a couple of hours later and did his best to hide his disappointment. He didn't play in the NatWest final either, and even though he was a member of the official party, we could see how badly he was taking it.

Steve was a good lad; tried his arse off for Lancashire. And there were times when he bowled very quick. But he never found a good English length and he paid the price. I felt sorry for him. He was in a no-win situation as a one-year stand-in for Waz, and it just never worked out for him.

Danny Morrison was the same in 1992. Now Danny was a very useful performer, and only Richard Hadlee has taken more than his 160 wickets in 48 Tests for New Zealand. Like Steve, he arrived as a stand-in for Waz. And like Steve, he never lived up to our expectations of him. We could never quite work out why. He was a swing bowler who kept the ball up to the bat. And even though he was only a little guy, he was deceptively quick. That was part of the problem at first. The slips stood too close, chances went down and Danny's confidence suffered. As a bowler you are always looking to get your wicket tally up and running early doors and it didn't help that so many catches were shelled off his bowling. By the time we really worked out where to stand, the wickets had flattened out and he was struggling.

Danny was a great lad in the dressing-room, though. Daft as a brush and always ready to play a leading role in the pranks and banter. There has never been a shortage of those two qualities at Old Trafford. And there hasn't been a Lancashire player in all my years on the staff who hasn't had to take his turn. Mike Watkinson once did me something rotten with a box full of those little polystyrene shells that are used to protect breakables. I don't know what the original contents of the box were and I don't care. I just know that for three months after Winker dumped those shells in my coffin, I spent the best part of my life trying to get rid of them. They were everywhere. I cleaned my coffin out every week, washed all my gear time and again and week after week, I was absolutely certain I'd finally solved the problem. Then I'd come into the tent after a hard day out in the middle, take my boots off and a dozen of those bloody shells would come rolling out. I whittled the suspects down to two or three and finally managed to force Watky into a confession.

Of course, that put him on his guard for my revenge, so I had to bide my time and wait for the right moment. It came at Derby a few weeks down the road. It's amazing how often the County Ground at Derby has loomed large in my legend – either on the field or, as in this case, in the form of a dressing-room joke. And it was all down to a couple of packets of ginger nuts.

After the morning warm-up, there is always a pot of tea and some biscuits waiting for the players and on this particular occasion it was ginger nuts. As usual, no one wanted to know about the biscuits, so I quietly snaffled them and stashed them away in my bag. If anyone noticed, they didn't say anything. I managed to find a quiet moment when the rest of the players were on the dressing-room balcony and nipped back inside, where I unwrapped the ginger nuts and stuffed them, one by one, behind the knee roll of Watky's pads. I then threw away the wrappers and went back out to rejoin the lads. Not a word to anyone.

Now, regular watchers of Lancashire down the years will know that it isn't exactly unusual for Watky to be rapped on the pads. So it was inevitable that the ginger nuts came in for quite a battering. But after a week or so, he still hadn't said a word about stray biscuits in his pads. He either hadn't noticed, or he had quietly cleared them all out and kept quiet about it. I decided to investigate and sure enough, the biscuits were still there, undisturbed but well down on their luck.

The more Winker netted, the more he was hit on the pads and the more the ginger nuts crumbled. A couple of weeks after I'd done the deed, Mike had a decent knock out in the middle and I was in the dressing-room when he returned. It was a hot day and the pads had taken the usual pounding on the outside and were a bit hot and sweaty inside. I didn't fancy the biscuits' chances of staying undetected. Mike came in, unstrapped the pads and there, all down the front of his trousers, was a beige stain made up of soggy crumbs. Watky looked at the stain and then looked at me. I looked at the stain and then back at Watky.

'I don't know what's happening, Oscar. I've had these brown stains on the front of my bloody trousers every day for about the last three weeks. I just can't work it out.'

I solemnly inspected the two stains. 'Bloody hell, you're right. I've never seen owt like it.' I shrugged, looked suitably bemused and ambled out of the room, trying desperately not to laugh. As I looked back, Winker was still inspecting the stains, shaking his head in disbelief.

A couple of weeks later we were playing a Sunday League game at Old Trafford. We netted beforehand and Watky was last to bat. Before fielding practice he came into the dressing-room, took his pads off, threw them down on to his coffin and got up to join in the practice session. As he did so, a ginger nut rolled across the dressing-room floor. We both watched, transfixed, as it came to a halt under one of the benches. 'Where the fuck did that come from?' he exclaimed. I couldn't speak for laughing. Watky picked up one of his pads, inspected both sides, gave it a shake and then put his hand behind the knee roll. Out came this brown mass of congealed ginger nuts. When Mike saw me doubled up laughing, it dawned on him who the culprit might be. One to Oscar. I'm not normally one of the main pranksters, but that will always go down as one of my better ones.

There are a few more up my sleeve for the next time I cop a couple myself from one of the younger lads like Andrew Flintoff. At the moment, it's all fairly obvious stuff from Flinty. Shoelaces tied together, socks snipped, that kind of thing. But he's only young. No doubt he'll mature with age.

I suppose if I had to pick out my biggest mate down the years, it would have to be Warren Hegg. We joined the staff together and we've grown up together. I've spent more time with him than anyone else, on the field, on the golf course, socially. We've always roomed together and Warren has somehow managed to survive the experience relatively unscathed.

He's one of those people who can nod off to sleep at any time of day or night. If Chucky isn't around in the dressing-room, it's a pound to a penny he'll have found a quiet corner and dozed off for half an hour. He is well up the batting order in the World XI of sleepers. And when we're away on the circuit, he likes his lie-in. Now I've always been the exact opposite. I'm up and about bright and early, into the shower and off and running for the day ahead. I could never be doing with the sight of Warren still fast asleep at 7.30 a.m. I'd try to wake him up, tell him we had to be down at breakfast by 8.00 or 8.30 or whatever. He never took a blind bit of notice. But I sorted him out in the end.

In the old days, I always used to carry a ghetto blaster around with me. Wherever I went, so did the blaster. It was about the only chance I had to listen to a bit of decent music. The Stranglers were my speciality. Anyway, one morning I decided I'd had enough of Warren hanging around in bed and opted for direct action. I put a Sex Pistols tape in the blaster, turned the volume up to full, moved the machine safely out of arm's reach, pressed play and belted into the shower. It was deafening even in there and it didn't take Warren long to locate the source of the racket and leap out of bed and, amid a torrent of oaths directed towards the bathroom, switch off the blaster.

From then on, whenever I thought it was time for an alarm call, I had the blaster loaded up, ready for action. Mind you, Chucky got his own back eventually by replacing The Stranglers with his own bloody awful Kylie Minogue tapes.

We both know where the other is coming from, on and off the field.

If I've got a problem bowling, the first person I'll turn to for help will be Warren. He's seen more of me than anyone else and can usually spot where I'm going wrong. I trust his judgement. He's the same with his batting. I'm the man he turns to if there's a problem.

I suppose it would be nice to add that if either of us is going through a bad trot with the bat, the other one will be on hand to offer a spot of sympathy. Not a bit of it. The stick starts here! Chucky will pick up his bat and get ready to set off for the middle and I'll chip in: 'I'm just making a coffee, Warren. How many sugars do you want?' And if I'm out for a blob in the first innings, the main reason for wanting to get off the mark second dig is to avoid the flak that will be flying my way from Warren if I arrive back in the dressing-room with a pair to my name.

Nobody fails on purpose and we all know how much it hurts. We all want one another to succeed and we know that if we do badly, it will never be for want of trying. And believe me, there is no worse feeling than trekking back to the tent when you've been out for nought. But once you're back in, you can either hang around sulking or get over it by having a bit of a laugh and a joke. That's how Warren and I have always played it, and it's worked.

As a wicketkeeper, he's one of the top three. Has been for years. He first played in 1986 and his big chance came a year later when both John Stanworth and Chris Maynard were injured. He was only 19, but he seized his opportunity and has been there ever since. A fixture in the side. He's got great hands and a brilliant temperament.

George Duckworth has always been recognised as the greatest keeper Lancashire have produced and people reckoned no one would ever approach his record of 922 victims in 434 first-class appearances. But Warren won't be a million miles away from that by the time he packs it in.

It's a different game these days of course, because in Duckworth's time they played over 30 first-class games a season, while we have rarely gone above 20 since I started in 1987. Nowadays it's down to 16. But Warren's record stands comparison with Duckworth's. He currently has 637 catches and 76 stumpings to his name in 265 games and that's not counting his one-day figures. It's impossible to compare different eras and if Duckworth was the best, then so be it. But he must have been a bloody good keeper if he's any better than Warren.

Chucky has been so unlucky not to win many more caps than the couple he collected on the 1998 tour to Australia. Jack Russell has been *numero uno* for years now, but Warren and Stephen Rhodes of Worcestershire have been right at the top of the queue behind him. Both would have played much more international cricket if England hadn't opted to use Alec Stewart as a wicketkeeper-batsman and I'm sure Warren would have done the business in England's one-day side. After all, he's done it often enough for Lancashire, hasn't he? Like I said before, it was always asking too much of Alec to be captain, opener and wicketkeeper, and Warren should have been given his chance.

He's been a great cricketer for Lancashire, a great mate to me and long may it continue. Pete Martin is another good pal, and was the best man at my wedding. He was from Accrington originally and then the family moved over to Doncaster, which explains why he's so tight with his money! He is a great bowler who just keeps getting better – another player who's had a raw deal from England.

Chucky and Digger are both key members of the Lancashire Golf Society, which I formed a few years back. Most of the lads are keen golfers but there was always a bit of aggro over handicaps whenever we met up for a day out. Only a handful had official club handicaps and the rest thought of a number, doubled it and opted for that on the day. So I decided to make the job official. I opened a bank account, we all chucked 20 quid in as a float and I got to work on an official handicapping system. We have a couple of days out in the autumn and then more in the winter. Between us, we've got plenty of contacts at good courses who will give us a decent deal.

I'm one of the tigers with a handicap of five and if I play regularly, I'm pretty steady. If I haven't had a game for a few weeks, it's a touch of the Red Arrows. Glenn Chapple is the pick of the bunch but most of the boys are pretty useful. Basically, though, it's all a bit of fun and a good excuse for staying in touch out of season.

Like I say, we're all mates. But over a career, there will always be one or two players who fall out for one reason or another and there's bound to be friction. I suppose I could follow the fashion and point the finger at some of the famous players I've been involved with, and maybe earn myself a few quid and some tabloid headlines. But sorry folks, that's not my style. I've enjoyed just about every minute of my time at Lancashire and at this stage of my career, the last thing I want to do is dig the dirt about people who were, and still are, my friends.

12
A CLOUD OVER CRICKET

The sporting world missed a beat when, in April 2000, it was revealed that Hansie Cronje, captain of South Africa and his country's Mr Clean, had been involved in shady dealings with illegal bookmakers – and who knows how much more? No one was more stunned than Austin, a friend of the disgraced South African captain.

Not so long ago, people used to say they could tell you exactly where they were and what they were doing when they heard that President Kennedy had been shot. It was the same in a way for the cricketing world when the news came through that Hansie Cronje was in the dock.

It was Tuesday, 11 April 2000 when we learned that Hansie was being investigated over his involvement with illegal bookmakers and claims that he had been paid to give information about matches. The Lancashire squad had just returned from our pre-season tour of South Africa, where there had been absolutely no hint that anything of this nature was in the air. That Tuesday, we'd been having a morning workout at Old Trafford and when we got back to the dressing-room we heard the news. Nobody could believe it. Hansie? You must be joking. That was the unanimous verdict.

Hansie had always seemed squeaky clean. He was deeply religious, as well as being a rich man in his own right. The sums being bandied about would have meant damn all to a man with his bank balance. It just didn't add up that the captain of the South African cricket team would put his career, reputation and the rest of his life on the line like that. And big names from the cricket world queued up to say so. A day later, they were proved horribly wrong as Hansie started to confess.

Of course, no one was under any illusions about the possible existence of betting rings and match fixing and all that kind of thing. For years, there had been rumours about these things going on in India and Pakistan. The two Australians, Shane Warne and Mark Waugh, were rapped over the knuckles and fined after admitting that they had given information to a bookmaker on a tour of India. There were also allegations that various Australians had been on the receiving end of bribe offers from Pakistan players.

Along with all that, there seemed to be a round-the-clock inquiry into the problem in Pakistan itself, with all sorts of players' names, including our own Wasim Akram, dragged through the mire. In fact, it had become a bit of a standing joke with Waz during his Lancashire days. If he got a duck or bowled badly, it was only a matter of time before someone would ask how much the opposition had paid him to perform like that. Waz would just laugh about it, and have a go back. I've chatted to him more seriously about it once or twice and Waz always insisted he was not involved in any way. For the record, I believed him then and I believe him now. OK, so he wasn't completely cleared by the investigation that ended with Salim Malik and Ata-ur-Rehman being banned, but for my money Waz is straight.

Then along came Cronje. I know Hansie pretty well and he has always seemed a hell of a good bloke. We met up when I was part of the England squad for the Hong Kong Sixes three years ago. There was a team from each of the Test-playing countries involved and we were all staying in the same hotel. It was quite a social whirl, to put it mildly. The night we arrived, we were invited aboard a cruiser to take a trip round Hong Kong harbour, with eats and drinks supplied. The Asian teams politely turned down the invitation and the West Indies failed to show up, too. On past form, they'd probably all be asleep. But the cricketers of England, Australia, New Zealand and South Africa hit the party trail with a vengeance and we had a hell of a night out.

From then on, I spent a fair bit of time with Hansie and the other South African players, either at the ground or in the hotel and, like I say, he was a good guy, one of those people who would always help you out if you had a problem. If he spotted you in the hotel lobby or the restaurant or wherever, he'd come across and have a chat. He was captain of his country and one of the big names in the cricket world but as far as I was concerned on that tour, he was just Hansie Cronje, good mate.

As I said earlier on, we had a brief chat before England's game against South Africa in the 1999 World Cup and later in the competition, I asked Hansie if he'd mind having a few bats autographed by the South African side for my 2000 benefit year. No problem at all. Hansie disappeared with an armful of bats and returned soon afterwards with the job done.

So you can probably understand why I was more bewildered than most when the allegations came out, followed rapidly by Cronje's admission that he had been involved with illegal betting. Since then we've had a series of enquiries into betting and match fixing, a sorry story that will run and run. Who knows where the trail will lead. But it's important to separate the two distinct issues: one, taking money for giving information, and two, match fixing.

Cronje's first offence was supplying info to bookies in return for cash. That is wrong, very wrong. But in my book, it's still not a hanging offence. At a very basic level, you don't have to be Albert Einstein to know that in Bombay or Calcutta it's going to be warm and dry with no chance of rain, the pitch will be flat and it will take spin more and more as the game goes on. And nearer home, if anyone is prepared to give me 500 quid to switch on the teletext, read the weather forecast and tell them it's going to rain, then bring 'em all on! Just a joke. But come on, that's the kind of information people can find out for themselves, and why bookies should be trying to pay cricketers to provide it is beyond me. More fool them, I say. But if the bookies know the team line-ups in advance or what the skipper will do if he wins the toss, they are in pole position. Players should be punished if they accept money for supplying details like that. It's a stupid thing to do, but at least international players know the score now: if they're found out, they're in big trouble.

But what about your average county pro? What's he supposed to do when a punter comes over and asks how the pitch is going to play or who's fit or whether we'll be having a bat if we win the toss? It happens all the time. At the ground, in the hotel, down the local. And while no one is going to hand over money for that sort of info, how are we to know that it won't be passed on to a high-street bookie? Where do we draw the line?

I'm not so daft that I couldn't recognise an Indian bookie if he called me up from Bombay offering to pay me for telling him what Lancashire would do if we won the toss, or whether Neil Fairbrother would be fit to play in an important one-day semi-final. But if I'm down at Haslingden CC on a Sunday afternoon and a couple of people ask me whether I'll be fit to play for Lancashire in 48 hours, what do I say? I suppose I could turn round and tell them I was not allowed to give out that kind of information, and go down in their eyes as one of the greatest prats of all time. Or I could say: 'Aye, of course I'll be fit. No problem. I hope you'll be down there to cheer us on.' That's always been my reaction to that kind of question and as far as I know, no one has ever gone running off to the bookie on the strength of it. But now that the Cronje affair has exposed exactly what can go on, perhaps we should never trust anyone any more.

As far as I am aware, there have only been one or two isolated instances of English players being approached, and they were all rejected instantly and reported to the authorities. Apparently someone had a quiet word with Adam Hollioake when he was captain of the side in Sharjah a few years back. He immediately reported the incident to the tour officials. End of story. I am sure the remark by one of the bookies involved in the Cronje business that it was pointless to approach English players because they are too honest is true. If not, heaven help us.

The business of match fixing, though, is a whole new ball game. The possibility that matches are being fixed left, right and centre beggars belief, but it does make you think. After all, there have been some very dodgy results in international cricket over the last few years. I was always brought up to play the game hard but fair – may the better team win and all that. Perhaps that's an old-fashioned attitude, I don't know. But I just can't imagine anyone in the English game agreeing to fix a match for the benefit of the bookmakers. For starters, how would you set about it?

Let's bring it right back home and pretend that John Crawley, my own captain at Lancashire, has been bunged a king's ransom to throw a NatWest semi-final against Yorkshire. What does he do next? He can't throw a match on his own, can he? He has to have an absolute minimum of three more players on board – let's say a key batsman, an all-rounder and a vital bowler. Right, so he's signed up Neil Fairbrother, Andrew Flintoff and me. Then what? We've all got to perform badly. OK, that can be arranged. But what about the other seven? They aren't going to sit around and do nothing while the captain messes up his field placings, two of his bowlers throw down a load of rubbish and four batters foul up completely. All hell would be let loose.

Even if those four players play a complete nightmare of a game, the other seven would be perfectly capable of winning the match on their own. I could throw down a long hop outside the off-stump, the batsman would cream it into the covers – only to see a fielder pull off a tremendous diving catch. Hugs all round. But let's say that thanks to the ineptitude of two bowlers and some crazy decisions by the captain, the opposition still rattle up 231 for five. Game over? Not a bit of it. Athers and Sourav Ganguly are in the mood. They go out and stage an action replay of the National League partnership they shared against Somerset in July 2000, and put on 192 in 34 overs. It takes a hell of a lot to lose a match from there, however hard you try.

So unless I've been wandering around with my eyes and ears shut for the last 14 years or more, I'm convinced that the English game is clean on that score. But I could be naughty and bring in the subject of 'arranged' matches. You know the type of situation. A game might be going nowhere at the start of the final day and the captains put their heads together and come up with a fourth innings target. A few overs of 'deccy bowling' follow to set-up a declaration and an agreed run chase. A good day's cricket is had by all, and even the losers admit that it's been better than playing out a tame draw: like Cronje's decision to offer England a chance to win the final Test in South Africa last winter, although that result has subsequently been under scrutiny.

But hang on a minute. That contrived result could end up deciding the County Championship. It could earn one of the two sides a hefty slice of prize money and cost another team their share of the pot. It could mean the difference between promotion and relegation. And if, back at the start of the season, people have had a bet on one of the two sides involved to win the title, they could be quids in or out of pocket by the time the Championship is decided.

And all because of one arranged finish.

13
THE HOLY GRAIL

Pick up any copy of *Wisden* or the *Lancashire Cricket Yearbook* from the last ten years and you will read that, yet again, the Red Rose County has missed out on the County Championship champagne. Bringing the title back to Old Trafford for the first time in a generation has become an obsession. As the players prepared for the start of the 2000 season, they were only too aware that Lancashire's last outright success happened a very long time ago: 1934, to be precise.

I can understand everyone connected with Lancashire cricket having an obsession about the County Championship. After all, we're the biggest club in the land and we haven't won the title outright since 1934. That's a hell of a long time, and there aren't that many people around who can remember how it feels to win it. There was a joint Championship with Middlesex in 1950 but the bottom line is that the title has not landed in Red Rose territory for 66 years. That's too long.

The Championship has been top of the agenda for members and club officials every year I have been on the staff. As each year passes without the Championship pennant flying on top of the pavilion, the pressure is cranked up a notch or two. At the end of every season, no matter how well we have performed in the one-day competitions, we have been asked: 'Why didn't you win the Championship? Why didn't you do better? Why can't you play proper cricket as well as the one-day stuff? Why was it so near but so far again?' Why, why, why? And it starts again as soon as we put our heads over the parapet again six months later. 'Is this going to be THE year? Will you do it this time?'

Before the start of the 2000 season we had the annual press call, where the papers, television and radio come along to take their pictures and talk to the players about the season ahead. And as usual, the 64,000 dollar question was: 'Could this be your season for the Championship at long last?' When they spoke to the press and did their radio and TV interviews, the chairman, coach and captain were all asked to go public on our Championship chances. They all said that in their view, the 2000 squad was ideally equipped to finally do the business.

What do the players think? How have we approached each season, knowing that the County Championship is the Holy Grail for just about everyone involved at any level with Lancashire County Cricket Club? Is it the ultimate obsession for the men who have to go out there and win enough games to finally clinch the title? Frankly, no. We don't sit down during the pre-season build-up and say: 'We haven't won the Championship outright since 1934, so this year we are going to put all our efforts into that. Forget the one-day competitions, we'll toss them away. It's Championship or bust.' That would be madness. There are four major competitions out there and we start the season aiming to win every game in every competition. Impossible? Yes. But only until that first defeat or draw comes along. We don't try and look at our strengths and weaknesses and work out where we might be in with a chance and where we'll be struggling. We're in there to win them all.

Gradually as the season develops, our priorities change. We might miss out in the Benson & Hedges qualifying rounds. One down, three to go. Then we might be struggling a bit in the National League. Realistically, that's two down and two to go. We make a bit of progress in the NatWest so that's still in the frame and we're putting together a useful Championship run. Still two down, two to go. Then, after winning a NatWest quarter-final, we're rolled over in a couple of county games and slip down the table a bit. One and a half to go. And so it goes on.

Hopefully, by the time the kit goes into the bag for the last time in the middle of September, one of those dreams has come true and there is some silverware in the cabinet. Better still if there's more than one trophy floating about. But there's no way we can start a season putting everything into one particular competition. It just wouldn't make sense. The nearest we came to doing that was back in the 1998 season, Dav

Whatmore's second as coach. Like I said before, Dav struggled to come to terms with the requirements of the English game at first, but he learned fast and by the time he sat down with the senior players for a pre-season meeting at the beginning of his second year, he knew all about the Championship obsession at Old Trafford.

'Right boys, how many games do we need to win to be sure of the Championship?'

A general shrug.

'Come on, you must have some idea. How many wins will it take?'

'Ten will get you close; if we win 11, we'll take the title. No problem.'

Another pause for thought.

'OK, let's look at the fixtures. Where are we going to get those 11 victories from?'

Yet another thoughtful silence while we all studied our fixture lists.

'Well, we start with Sussex away. Should win that one. Then Middlesex at home. Another win. Kent, Essex and Northants away. Mark us down for one win out of three. Somerset at home? Go on then, a win. Then it's Surrey at our place. Tough.' We came up with seven likely victories.

'So, that's the first seven. Our bankers. Right, now let's look at the other ten and see where those last four wins are coming from.'

'Well, we'll see the Yorkies off, even though it's at Headingley . . . ' And so it went on. Eventually, we came up with 11 key games that we simply had to win.

What happened? It poured down for most of that first game at Hove and after two declarations to contrive a finish, Sussex got home with two balls and two wickets to spare. First banker shot down. Then Middlesex arrived at Old Trafford. It pissed down on three of the four days. A draw. Bang goes another banker. So much for advance planning! In the end, we put a really strong run together from around the halfway mark, won a few of the dodgy ones and went very close. At the start of the final round of matches, it was between Leicester, us and Surrey. And Surrey and Leicester were playing one another. But Leicester absolutely hammered them from the first few overs, and from very early on in our game against Hampshire we were playing for second place. We got home by 161 runs and finished runners-up. How many games had we won? Eleven – our pre-season target. The only trouble is, so did Leicester. But they didn't lose any and collected a few more bonus points into the bargain. So we missed out again. All that planning flew out of the window. Back to the drawing board. The fans had to settle for the NatWest Trophy and the Sunday League instead.

We finished second in 1999 as well. But this time Surrey won 12 games, four more than anyone else, including Lancashire, and had the Championship sewn up early doors. And runners-up yet again in 2000. So the quest goes on . . .

In my time as a first-team player since 1987, Lancashire have finished second, ninth, fourth, sixth, eighth, twelfth, thirteenth, tenth, fourth, fifth, fifteenth, eleventh, second, second and second. We have also won 11 one-day trophies. To some extent, I would accept that there have been times when our one-day success has worked against us in the Championship. Batsmen have tried to play too many shots too soon; bowlers have tried to peg people back rather than take wickets. And when the wickets haven't come along, we've tried to experiment a bit and all of a sudden, the opposition are up and away. But generally speaking in the last few years we've definitely played better Championship cricket without our one-day game suffering too much. We've learned to separate the two far better and have proved we can be successful at both. It's all part of our changing approach to the game.

Eventually the Championship will come back to Old Trafford: the sooner the better. No one will be more delighted than me when it finally happens. But let's not forget that in the last decade of the old millennium, Lancashire won no fewer than eight one-day trophies, six of them in Lord's finals. We didn't do badly then, did we? Surely no one out there would have swapped all that silverware for a single Championship trophy.

PART FOUR

THE 2000 SEASON

14
THE COUNTDOWN

Austin's first season on the Lancashire staff began with evening indoor nets and a couple of beers in February. Now, as one of Lancashire's contracted players, he is on duty for the club all year round. As preparations get under way for the start of the first season of the new millennium, things certainly ain't what they used to be.

Sometimes, it's hard to believe how things have changed since I started. We thought we were highly professional back in 1986. But compared to the way we build up for a new season these days, we were just playing at it. Full-time contracts have obviously played a major part, although changes were taking place long before Lancashire offered us year-round deals from the start of the 1998 season. There had been a few rumours that it might happen and then towards the end of the 1997 season, we sat down with the management and sorted out the nuts and bolts of it. Basically, instead of being free agents between October and March, we are now committed to Lancashire 12 months a year. No more trying to find work in the winter, no more worries about the dole queue for the younger lads – and some of the older ones, for that matter. So on the face of it, it was a good idea. Just like a proper job, I suppose. During the winter, we were to have three days a week training and two days of vocational work.

Like anything else, though, there was a down side. The advantage of packing our bags in the autumn and returning to Old Trafford in spring was that we came back fresh and raring to go. In that first year of full-time contracts, it felt as if we'd never been away; we felt stale before a ball was bowled in anger.

We had wound down from the season at the beginning of October and were back in training at the start of December. It was a bit of a shock to the system, to put it mildly: de-icing the car and then running round the outfield in the pouring rain two weeks before Christmas to prepare for a season that didn't start until mid-April was never going to be a barrel of laughs. It wasn't long before the boys started to feel less than thrilled at the prospect.

While the vocational side was fine for the most part, there were times when it almost felt as if the club had to find things for us to do. A course in computer technology? Great. Not many of the lads even knew how to switch a computer on and this was a chance to get to know the basics. There was media training, sports psychology, talks about health, diet and nutrition. But not all the vocational stuff was exactly riveting, and that's me being diplomatic.

One way or another, it seemed as if we were spending all our time with Lancashire and cricket and not enough quality time at home. By the time we set off on tour to South Africa in the middle of March, we'd more or less had enough. And the tour was more of the same. When we returned home we were ready for a break, instead of feeling all fired up for the new season.

In the end we had a great year, of course, with two one-day trophies and second place in the Championship. So you could say that full-time contracts worked. But we were slow out of the blocks and I'm sure that was because we all felt a bit stale.

Next time around, we didn't have to report back until January and all in all, it felt better. There is a limit to how much physical work players can go through in 12 months. It's a hell of a hard season, a schedule of 16 four-day games, 16 one-dayers in the National League and anything up to 12 in the NatWest and the Benson & Hedges. Throw in all the travelling up and down the motorway and we're entitled to a spot of rest and recuperation by the time the season ends and, just as importantly, we need a chance to take things easy every now and then in the build-up to the season. Running around a gym for three hours, three days a week in February isn't necessarily the best preparation for spending six-and-a-half hours in the field on a hot day in July. In fact, how do you prepare players for that? Cricket is unique in that respect. Footballers are out there for 90 minutes, rugby players for 80 minutes and so on. For us, it can be over six hours of stop-start and more to come the next morning

Don't get me wrong, I'm not against full-time contracts. Far from it. But what we have in place at the moment is not yet the finished article and there is plenty of room for discussion about which direction we should be heading in. And to be fair to the club, they are good listeners. Both sides know there's some fine tuning still to be done, but there is give and take on both sides and between us, we'll get it right in the end.

As long as they keep us away from the Krypton Factor, our workout from hell. We went through that one before the start of the 1997 season, just when full time contracts were being mentioned as a possibility for the following year. Dav Whatmore decided a day out with the army on the Krypton Factor assault course at Holcombe Moor near Blackburn would tone us up nicely. Dav was heavily into something called SAQ training: Speed, Agility, Quickness. We'd already been running around Old Trafford with parachutes strapped to our backs before we arrived for our day out at Holcombe Moor. Day out? One long nightmare, more like. It started with a three-mile cross-country run, complete with press-ups and sit-ups every five minutes. Then the assault course itself, scrambling under nets, over fences, through streams, everything you need to prepare yourself for a long day in the field. When we finally dragged ourselves back into the changing-room, the kit went into the rubbish bin and we went into the showers. The verdict: if this is a sample of what life's going to be like with full-time contracts, forget it!

At least we were able to get away to South Africa on tour after that. It gave us a chance to play a bit of proper cricket out in the sunshine. Pre-season tours have come in all shapes and sizes since that first trip to Jamaica in 1987. We've been all over the place: Australia, South Africa, Zimbabwe, North Yorkshire, North Wales, Portugal. We've even played football at Eden Gardens, Calcutta. That happened in 1997, when we were invited out to India to take part in a match commemorating the centenary of a clothing company with connections in Manchester. In January. Obviously, we'd had no serious preparation before we flew out for what we were led to believe would be no more than a one-day bunfight, a bit like a benefit match. We stayed overnight in Delhi and snatched a few hours' sleep before we were knocked up to catch the early morning flight to Calcutta.

We were staying in one of the best hotels in town. We had 24 hours to acclimatise, and then reported to Eden Gardens for a net the day before the match. But it was pretty lethargic stuff, and it wasn't long before the football came out, temporary goalposts were erected and the serious stuff began. We were just starting to turn it on a bit for the benefit of a handful of intrigued onlookers when we spotted the entire hierarchy of Eden Gardens racing across the outfield towards us.

'You can't do that here!'

'Can't do what here?'

'You can't play football at Eden Gardens.'

We could and we did – as far as I know, our warm-up match remains the only game of football ever played on the hallowed turf. To top it all, we won the cricket, too. But that's another story.

Like I say, we were under the impression that the game would be a very light-hearted affair, either against the Bengal side that played at Eden Gardens in the East Zone of the Ranji Trophy, or possibly an All Stars XI, looking to give the fans a spot of festival-style cricket. No way! When we saw the opposition line-up in the paper, it looked ominously like an India Second XI. Names like Robin Singh, Kambli, Jadeja and Joshi were among the chosen few. And the report suggested that they weren't just there for the ride. They weren't, either. It was deadly serious stuff, but somehow we managed to win it and collect our first trophy of the season.

There were little cut-glass tankards for all the players and a two-day stop-off in Delhi on the way back. Apart from one or two cases of the dreaded Delhi belly, it was the perfect way to wind down from the festive season and a great chance to sample Indian cuisine. Right from the word go, we worked on the basis of when in India, eat Indian. We didn't fancy our chances on steak and chips or pasta. And we were right.

If I had to plump for the best pre-season tour venue of the lot, it would probably be Portugal. While the choice of the Algarve as a pre-season destination for cricketers sounded a bit odd at first, it turned out to be just about perfect. OK, the net facilities were not exactly top-notch, but I've always believed there's more to pre-season tours than netting, fitness and cricket practice. They are important, of course, but there's also the question of team bonding. We're like a family. If 15 or 16 blokes are going to live in one another's pockets for six months, it's essential they get on well. There has to be a whole lot of give and take. It's a long season and a bitchy dressing-room never wins trophies. Team spirit is absolutely vital. Three weeks in Portugal in March was perfect on that score. We were up early, put in the hours on the practice ground and then went off to the golf course every afternoon. I've never known the boys so relaxed.

The trip to Tasmania in 1991 was a good one, too. It was there that I found out the hard way that you don't get David Boon out leg before on his home patch. We were playing an Invitation XI at the Bellerive Oval and Boonie came in number three as usual. He was soon into his stride, smacking us all round the ground. David Hughes brought me on when he'd been batting for a few overs and straight away, I rapped him on the pad, bang in front. Not out. Two balls later, I hit the pad again. He was on the back foot and this time it would have knocked all three out. Everybody went up. Boon never batted an eyelid. Not out, said the umpire. Next ball, Boonie nudged it towards third man and trotted down the wicket with a big grin on his face. 'Hold your breath, Oscar, mate. You've more chance of getting Javed Miandad leg before in Karachi than me in Tasmania.' Ah well, at least we knew from then on!

He went on to score the inevitable ton, despite being caught on the boundary a couple of times. At the Bellerive there's this dirty great tree right on the edge, and twice Boonie launched one into the tree and a fielder was waiting underneath to take the catch. That's out in my book, but each time the umpire signalled six before the ball dropped out of the tree and the catch could be taken.

All good stuff on a pre-season tour, and after the game there was a benefit dinner for our tormentor-in-chief, with his Australian teammate Merv Hughes as guest speaker. The mayor and mayoress were there and so were the Tasmania players' wives. So it was embarrassing, to say the least, when Merv started effing and blinding all over the place and recounting lurid tales of the Aussies' exploits in and out of bed on various overseas tours. No one knew where to look and it was a huge relief when Merv finally sat down.

Graham Lloyd took advantage of the break to nip for a pee and he was just emerging from the gents when Graeme Fowler leapt on him from behind. Typical Foxy. Unfortunately, Bumble was on a final warning after causing a rumpus in the hotel corridor a couple of nights earlier and Yozzer was first on the scene as he gave Foxy what for. 'Right Lloyd, that's it. First plane home tomorrow. I've had a bellyful of you on this tour.' Fortunately, he'd forgotten all about the incident the following morning.

The only down side to that Tasmanian trip was that it happened to coincide with Easter. In Tasmania, everything shuts down for the Easter weekend. And I mean everything. We finished a practice game and went into the bar for a drink – and it was shut. Why? Easter. Back to the hotel for a shower, down to the bar. Shut. That's right, Easter. So was every restaurant in town, and the hotel restaurant. We couldn't get a bite to eat. The only beer around was in the room minibars, and that didn't last long. We ended up stocking up with bread rolls for the whole day at breakfast and persuading the cricket club barman to open up and sell us a few cases to keep in the minibar. Our only entertainment was a nightly golf tournament in the hotel corridor.

Since those days, though, tours have become more and more intense and there's far less time for fooling about. In fact, there's far less time for anything except cricket. This year's trip to South Africa was our fourth visit to Capetown in a row and to be honest it's all becoming a bit too familiar. Same place, same facilities, same everything. And each year, there is more cricket and less relaxation.

The season starts here . . .

**15
APRIL**

For Lancashire, the first season of the new millennium gets under way on Friday 7 April with a three-day friendly against Cambridge University at Fenners. The players, fresh from their pre-season tour to South Africa, head south after meeting the media at the annual press call at Old Trafford the day before the game. It is the first time new coach Bob Simpson has been involved in the selection process. To everyone's surprise Austin, who will chronicle Lancashire's season month-by-month, is not included in the squad for the first game of his Benefit year.

Not being included in the squad didn't really bother me, to be honest. I've never read too much into University games. It's good to get a match under your belt early on, but hamstring strains are easy to come by early in the season. You bowl half-a-dozen overs, spend a couple of hours wrapped in three sweaters on the boundary edge and then come back for a second spell when you've thoroughly cooled down. Bad news. Even so, it would have been good to get outdoors for three days after being forced to spend the best part of two weeks desperately trying to get outside instead of working in the indoor nets. We hardly had a flake of snow all winter, spent three weeks in Capetown and never saw a cloud. Then on our first day back at Old Trafford, I looked out of the window and sure enough, there was a bit of white fluffy stuff on the lawn. By the time I reached the main road it was snowing like hell. Typical! Some of the lads had to dig their cars out. Welcome to the cricket season.

For me, it was the start of the big one. My Benefit Year. It began on 1 January and there had been seven dinners and three sports forums by the time the players set off without me for that first game at Fenners, with another seven dinners, nine golf days, four cricket matches, two clay pigeon shoots and a couple of Caribbean nights still to come later this year. No doubt a few more functions will be slotted in along the way.

I had no illusions. I knew from the start that it was going to be a busy year, on and off the field. But under the England and Wales Cricket Board rules, the beneficiary is not allowed to play an active part in raising money through Benefit donations; it all has to be done through a Benefit committee. And as a beneficiary is only as good as his chairman and committee, I invited John Cotton round for a meal last December, plied him with good food and strong drink and then popped the question: 'Will you be my chairman?' I've known John for a long time. We come from the same background, speak the same language, call a spade a spade. John later claimed he couldn't remember agreeing to my proposal but once he had cleared it with Thwaites Brewery, his employers, he has given it 100 per cent. I know I'm going to be eternally grateful at the end of the year.

There's a bush telegraph about what kind of functions are going down well, and each beneficiary tries to come up with a few original ideas. John has organised a shipment of Australian wine, white and red, and has designed a special Ian Austin Benefit Year label for the bottles. I'll be seeing plenty of those over the next few months. The committee have sorted out a Benefit logo – it's like an Oscar statuette with a bull's head on top. There are also Ian Austin Benefit golf clubs, ties and caps: all sorts of things which can be 'bought' with a donation to the Benefit fund. And, of course, a 100-page Benefit brochure. On top of that there's a load of bats, stumps, shirts and other pieces of memorabilia which will be auctioned at dinners, golf days and all the other functions. Again, I have no part to play in that; I just have to sit around and let John, the committee and my teammates get on with it. Although I will be available for a bit of lifting if they need to ship a few cases of wine around for a dinner!

The beneficiary relies entirely on a huge amount of goodwill from many different people: his chairman and committee; the sponsors and all the others who agree to run a Benefit function and donate a sum from the proceeds to the fund; the thousands of people who attend the functions; guest speakers and celebrities; and supporters who put their money in the match day collection buckets. I just hope I'm not getting clattered all over Old Trafford when the announcement goes out over the PA system that 'a collection will shortly be held in aid of Ian Austin's Benefit'.

Then there are the other players. I know from experience that sometimes the last thing a player wants to do after he's arrived home from Brighton at 3 a.m. is get up at 8 a.m. on his day off to go and play in a Benefit match or golf day 100 miles up the road. You want to have some time with the wife and kids, sort out all those little bits of admin that have built up while you've been on the road for ten days. But you do it. Why? Firstly because the beneficiary is a mate, and secondly because one day, you hope, you'll be asking him to return the favour, if you're lucky and are awarded a Benefit. And that's one of the problems with the system. It was designed to reward a player for long service and loyalty, but there have been a hell of a lot of loyal cricketers who have missed out.

Sometimes, the beneficiary is a big-name international star who's got plenty of money in the bank anyway. Now don't get me wrong, I don't begrudge the top players the rewards that are now available – even if they are just a pittance compared with the kind of money professional footballers can earn. But the Benefit system was designed to reward the journeyman pro and not the superstar. There is a very real danger that in the next few years, the big names are going to clean up. We all rely on sponsors for our Benefit functions and if you're top man at a large business concern, whose dinner or golf day are you going to back? An England star, or a guy who's hacked around the county circuit for ten years? No contest, I'm afraid. So in my book, we need to be looking at a way of ensuring that all players receive some kind of retirement payment.

I believe the counties should be responsible for running a benefit fund each season. With the help of the players, who all have a network of contacts, they would organise the golf days, the celebrity cricket matches, the dinners and the forums. And, again with the help of the players if need be, find the sponsors. All the money raised would go into a pool for the playing staff. It would be totted up at the end of each year and put into a retirement fund for each player – let's say £2,000 for uncapped players and £5,000 for capped players. So if you're lucky enough to still be around after two years' uncapped service and another 12 years as a capped player, there's £64,000 plus accrued interest waiting for you when it's time to call it a day. That's not a fortune and it's less than most players would hope to raise from a Benefit, but it has the virtue of being fair because there would be something for every county cricketer. Not just the lucky few.

BULLY FOR YOU, OSCAR

What's more, young players who give up the prime years of their working life to play county cricket, the years when they would otherwise be making their way in whatever job they choose, would not find themselves struggling against the odds if they didn't make it. Every year, counties release players who have given several years' service and all they have to show for it is their savings from what is not exactly the best paid job in world sport. Surely it would make more sense if there was some kind of nest egg for them to fall back on. It's something we should be thinking about. Having said that, of course, the Benefit system is still in place and here and now I would like to say a big thank you to all the people who have helped me in any way or made donations to my fund so far and will be doing so between now and 31 December. Believe me, it means a hell of a lot.

Anyway, enough of the soap box, back to the cricket. After missing out at Cambridge, my season began when the Benson & Hedges qualifiers got under way against Notts at Trent Bridge on 15 April. It wasn't easy: we went into the game without an outdoor net and just a couple of centre-wicket practices. But we bowled well as a unit, kept it tight and won the game comfortably. A perfect start. We were off and running

The following day it was Yorkshire at Headingley, and the wheels came off. We were poor. The batting was average – we made 166 – but the bowling was terrible. We were all over the place, particularly myself and Pete Martin. Without boasting, Digger and I have been a bit of backbone of the team down the years, keeping it tight and giving nothing away, nicking the odd wicket here and there, putting the pressure on. But at Headingley it just didn't happen. Why not? Put it down to one of those days. The Yorkshire boys weren't much better, but at least they had the consolation of a win.

Two days later, we were at Durham. Sitting watching the rain come down. We hung on and hung on and eventually it stopped for long enough to have a ten-over thrash. The ground wasn't fit, to be honest. But we'll always back ourselves in those situations and we won easily.

We lost the plot at Derby, though. Again, we didn't get enough runs, although the lads said the pitch was doing a lot. Well, maybe it was for Derby, but it wasn't doing anything for us. I felt I was getting back into the old routine, but as a unit we didn't bowl well enough, and that's what it's all about. It's no good one or two lads bowling well if the others let it slide. You live and die as a unit. That's always been our motto at Lancashire.

It was all down to the final qualifier against Leicester at Old Trafford on

Easter Monday, and even then, we weren't certain to qualify if the results went against us. The bowling was much tighter but this time the batting let us down. When Mike Smethurst joined me with one wicket left, we still needed 25. Anyone who knows Smethers will agree that he's not the greatest bat in the world. In a team of number elevens he might scrape in at nine, ten or Jack, so the sight of him striding down the pavilion steps didn't fill me with confidence. But we had loads of overs left, he hung around and I farmed most of the strike. Eventually, Mike started opening out with flowing cover drives that ended up behind square leg and by the time he connected with a straight drive for four I knew we were on the way. Smethers will tell you we won it with a bit to spare.

People always say that I relish tough situations like that. OK, I've always enjoyed a good scrap but basically when it's down to the wire with the last man in, there's nothing to lose. If Smethers or me had got out, no one could have pointed the finger at either of us. Look at our top order: Atherton, Crawley, Ganguly, Fairbrother, Lloyd and Flintoff. All international batsmen. They should be winning games for us. It's no good blaming nine, ten and eleven because they get out at the death. Like I say, you just go out there and give it your best shot. Yes, we've got a useful late order: myself, Chucky, Pete Martin, Gary Yates and Glenn Chapple have all scored a first-class hundred. Chris Schofield will be scoring one before long, too. But the bottom line is that it's up to the batters to do the business on a regular basis. If they can't score at three or four an over it's no good expecting the tail to score at eight or nine.

Anyway, we made it. Back in the dressing-room, it was 'Well played, Bully. Go and collect your Gold Award.' And PS, you're not going to Canterbury for the Championship game against Kent.

It was a bitter disappointment. The coach told me there was a bit of concern about my fitness for a four-day Championship match. Blah, blah, blah. I'd be playing in a four-day Second XI game instead. It didn't add up. If I wasn't fit for the first team, why was I fit for the seconds? I wouldn't be doing anything different. There's not a lot you can say, though. I told Bob I wasn't happy and didn't agree with the reasons. He told me to go out there and get some runs and wickets and put a bit of pressure on him and that's exactly what I intend to do. But I can't pretend it wasn't a blow.

On top of everything else, my Mum has been taken into hospital. She has been suffering from cancer for some time and now we were told it might only be a matter of days.

BULLY FOR YOU, OSCAR

**16
MAY**

It will be the most traumatic month of Austin's life, a month when his cricket will fade into the background because of his mother's illness. A month of personal turmoil. And the little cricket he will play will only increase the tensions and frustrations of April.

Mum's illness overshadowed everything. We'd known for some time how desperately ill she was, but there was no way she was going to let go without a fight. The hospital would ring to say it might be an idea to get over there because it wasn't going to be long, but no sooner had she reached crisis point than she'd rally and we'd be back to square one. She hung on like that for over three weeks. Then the final call came to go up to the hospital. She was 60. In the end, it was a blessing. I didn't want her to carry on suffering like that and I know she didn't either. Talking to her a little while before, she let me know that she realised there was no way she was coming back and she wasn't going to go through the ordeal of a major operation just to survive until the next operation came around.

She and Dad had supported me from day one – and so had the washing machine! Over the wall at the back of our house was a school playing field, complete with a couple of trees that were perfect goal posts. At every available opportunity I was out there with my mates. Cricket in the summer, football in the winter, night after night. We'd be outside way after dark playing three-and-in or taking penalties. By the time we'd finished, our home-made goalmouth was a complete mudbath and we'd all be caked in mud from head to toe.

I'd nip back over the wall and Mum would spot me heading for the back door. 'Stop there! You're not coming in this house like that,' she'd shout, and out would come the hosepipe. I'd hose myself down until most of the mud had disappeared off me and my gear and then it was straight in the bath. Miraculously, my kit would be as good as new again the next morning, ready for another go. With four kids, the washing machine seemed to be constantly working, and there were four healthy appetites for Mum to satisfy every day.

Mum and Dad were always there in the early days at Haslingden and there was never any problem about transport to and from representative games when Lancashire started to take notice. They were more than happy to run me around and they'd stay and watch, see how I was doing. They carried on watching me all the way up the ladder. But they never tried to push themselves on me, never asked any favours. Sometimes I'd be having a chat with them about a game I'd played in a couple of days earlier and Mum would pick out a couple of incidents. They'd been there all the time without me knowing it, but hadn't wanted to make a fuss. They'd come along, enjoy the match and then clear off. When it came to a big game such as a Lord's final, a one-day semi and obviously my England début, I'd always make sure they had tickets and were properly treated, but apart from that they were happy just to do their own thing.

Mum never interfered when I decided to try and make a go of it in professional cricket. I don't know whether or not she thought it was risky and I ought to get some other qualifications under my belt first. All she said was that if I wanted to be a cricketer, she would support me all the way. And she did. When a few league clubs wanted me to go and pro with them in 1986, she was happy to leave the decision to me and so was Dad. We met the club representatives together, but in the end they both said that I had to decide for myself. Good advice. They never pushed me into anything, but I knew they were always there when I needed them.

Mum's funeral was on my birthday, 30 May. A fitting end to a month that will not go down in the Austin Hall of Fame. It had started OK, with a Benson quarter-final against Durham at Old Trafford. The wicket was doing a bit and we bowled them out reasonably cheaply with a much better bowling display. Then it was all fall down again. This time we found ourselves at 35 for five and staring straight down both barrels with well over a hundred still needed. Harvey and Chucky turned it round, Chris Schofield got a few and then it was left to me and Harvey to see us home. We were in the semi-final, against Gloucester at Bristol. The holders. Tough.

After beating Durham, there was another round of 'Well played, Bully.' And yet another quiet word: 'You won't be with the first team for the Championship game at Durham.' A real body blow. If a seam bowler like me could choose two places to play early season, one would be Canterbury and the other Chester-le-Street. I missed out on both.

Sure enough, conditions at The Riverside were perfect. Glenn Chapple took seven in the first innings, Mike Smethurst seven in the second. It was an ideal way to get the season up and running; a few wickets in the bank early doors is what all bowlers look for. But what do you do in these situations? Sit tight and get on with it. There's no point feeling sorry for yourself. But with a Benefit Year and the start of the new two-division set-up, it should have been an exciting time for me. Instead, I was on the outside looking in at Lancashire as far as Championship cricket was concerned and there were big problems on the home front. Not fair? Maybe not. But life isn't fair at times.

If I wasn't going to be playing first team cricket, it was obviously important to get some games under my belt with the Second XI. But one way or another, that didn't work out either. I couldn't play against Yorkshire at Crosby because I was involved in the Benson quarter-final. The following week, the seconds were due to play Hampshire down at Southampton while the first team had a free week. Assuming I'd be involved with the first team, we'd fixed up three Benefit functions and as I also needed to be near to home in case anything happened to my mum, the club agreed to let me miss that trip to Hampshire.

I spent that week going quietly round the twist. There were the daily visits and frequent phone calls to and from the hospital. As if that wasn't enough, I was rushing around for the Benefit, a dinner at Manchester United, a golf day at Rossendale and a cricket match at St Helens, all in the space of three days. I also had a book to be getting on with. And a family.

The following week the Second XI were due to play Middlesex at Blackpool and I was pencilled in for that one. But Mum passed away the day before the game so I withdrew from the side. The club were great about it. They told me that the family problems came first, and all I had to do was keep in touch and let them know if I was going to be available for the semi-final at Bristol on 28 May. I talked it over with my family and they all told me to do it. We'd fixed the funeral for the week after the game, and they said Mum would have wanted me to play – I'm sure they were right. I made myself available to the captain and the coach and Bob said straight away: 'Right, if you're available, your name's on the teamsheet.' I was hoping for a net on either the Thursday or the Friday before we set off for Bristol. But both days it was chucking it down, so I bowled at Mike Atherton for a while in the indoor school instead. It was OK, but not the real thing.

The journey down to Bristol was a nightmare. Five-and-a-half hours worth of Bank Holiday traffic. We should have had a net when we arrived but guess what? The heavens opened. They stayed open all night and when we arrived at the ground on Sunday morning there were three or four inches of water around the square and only one possible decision: no play.

So there I was on the Monday morning, bowling for Lancashire in a Benson semi-final with no serious outdoor cricket behind me for three weeks – not the ideal preparation. But as I've said, cricket is played between the ears and if you know your game plan and back yourself to do the business, it doesn't matter how much cricket you've played. I'm a well-organised cricketer and despite all the huge problems, I knew in my own mind what I had to do. People came up to me afterwards and said it was incredible that after losing my mum and playing no cricket at all, I could produce figures of one for 17 from ten overs in three separate spells. The words 'mental strength' were bandied about. If that's how people want to see it, then fine. But to me, I was doing my job.

Of course, there were some strong emotions involved. I don't deny that. I wanted Lancashire to win for my mum. I wanted to give Dad a trip to Lord's and a weekend in London. But sadly, it didn't work out. At half-time we were not displeased; at one point it looked as if Gloucester might get away a bit and make 260. Instead, we held it at 220 for six and they can't have been happy with that. It was an in-between sort of score. If a side has that many wickets in hand, they should be scoring 250-plus, and the Gloucester boys knew it. We reckoned we could get them, but losing three quick wickets put us right behind the eight-ball and we just slid further and further away from the required run rate. We didn't bat well again.

It was the story of our Benson & Hedges Cup 2000 – and there are only so many times you're going to get out of jail. When I went out to bat at 163 for seven with a handful of overs left it was basically a lost cause, bar a miracle. But miracles don't come along too often against a side like Gloucester. They've got their game sorted. They strangle you. They bowl straight, they don't give you any width to free your arms and have a swing. Jack Russell stands up to the medium pacers so you can't go down the track. It's difficult enough when you've got a reasonable target in your sights, but at eight or nine an over near the end it's impossible. We finished 15 short but it might as well have been 150. We were never really going to get them. It was a bitter disappointment.

So we're out of one competition already, and we're struggling a bit in the National League. We've got games in hand but we need to string some results together. And we could do with something other than rained-off draws in the Championship. The NatWest starts for us in June, so it's going to be an important month all round. We're going to have to pick up the tempo a bit: we need more runs from the top order in all the competitions and the bowlers have got to be more consistent. We'll have to manage without Digger, though. He broke his thumb in the Championship game against Derbyshire at the end of the month, and right now it's touch and go whether he'll bowl another ball for us this season. Certainly he'll be doing nothing before the middle of August – a huge blow.

Here endeth May, you might say. A rotten end to a pretty awful month. Surely things can only get better now. And from a personal point of view, can I play some cricket, please?

17 JUNE

Can he play any cricket? Not a lot! In the first three weeks of the month, Austin features in Lancashire's only County Championship game, a NatWest Trophy tie against a minor county and three National League matches. The third, a day-night game against Northants Steelbacks under the Old Trafford floodlights, turns out to be an occasion he is unlikely to forget for a long time.

Problems with the floodlights. There was a bit of a gale blowing so it was touch and go whether it would be safe for us even to make a start. A Duckworth-Lewis finish loomed. We won the toss and stuck them in. As per usual, I was bowling into Hurricane Stretford. We needed to keep it tight from my end and fire away from the other. At the end of my second over, I started to feel discomfort in my right calf. Nothing definite, just a bit of a niggle. The sort that usually goes away.

The first three balls of the third over were no problem. After the fourth, my calf was a bit tender again and with the glorious gift of hindsight, I should have stopped there and then. I didn't. Fifth ball, I ran in as usual, let it go and felt a searing, stabbing pain. I crumpled in a heap. It took me a while to sit up, never mind bowl. Lawrie Brown came on and got me back on my feet, but I could hardly walk. Obviously, it was game over for me. The trouble was, we were a bit short in the bowling department and if anyone had come on and bowled the last ball of my third over, that single ball would have counted as one of his allowance of nine. That might have caused problems for the skipper, juggling the bowling around at the end. So I told John I'd struggle through with that one ball. I started with a run-up of two yards – no chance. One yard. No better. I opted for standing at the crease, bringing my arm over and just getting the bloody ball down the other end somehow. It wasn't easy, not least because most of the Lancashire fielders and Mal Loye, who was facing, were killing themselves with laughter. I stood still and turned my arm over; Mal was laughing so much he couldn't do anything other than push it straight back to me. And that was that. Dot ball, and the end of my cricket for the foreseeable future.

It was a hell of a blow. I'd started June determined to put all the personal problems of May behind me as best I could and finally get on with some cricket. Things went well at first; I hadn't been chosen for the Championship game against Derby at Old Trafford, but when Digger broke his thumb I drew the short straw and was called on to do the Twelfth Man duties. I was back in the line-up for the National League game at Northampton on the first Sunday of the month – another poor performance, another defeat. Once again, we didn't score enough runs. Batting first, we only made 187 for six and couldn't defend it. For one reason or another, it was only our third game in the competition and we were still looking for our first win.

Even at that early stage, our shortage of runs was becoming a major worry. On paper, we have one of the best top sixes in the game . . . but I've never been one to talk about strengths and weaknesses on a piece of paper. I like to see good results in the newspaper the next day. And as far as the National League is concerned, we just haven't been firing from day one.

After the Northants disappointment, I got the nod for the four-dayer against Hampshire at Liverpool, my first Championship game of the season. With Digger out, there was obviously going to be an opportunity for someone and I made sure the powers-that-be knew I was in the frame. I'd asked Bob why I wasn't in the side, what I needed to do to get in; the usual gripes and groans from any cricketer on the circuit when he isn't in the line-up. It must have worked. We did well, too; beat 'em in two days. We played some good cricket, while Hampshire were pretty poor. From a personal point of view I was happy with my bowling. I started off with five overs off the reel into another gale in the first innings and the idea was to keep rotating the bowlers in short spells from that end. Instead, I never got back on because we bowled

Hampshire out for 95. I had two longer spells in the second innings and picked up a couple of wickets. I finished with two for 23 from 19 overs, with 13 maidens. The ball was coming out well. I felt good.

I expected to stick around for the next four-day game, against New Zealand A the following week, also at Liverpool. But when I turned up on the morning of the match, I was told my services would not be required. Chris Schofield had been left out of the England party for the Edgbaston Test against the West Indies and he was given a game instead.

Normally, I would have no problem with that. Friendly games against touring A teams are not exactly the flavour of the month with most county pros, and I wouldn't be giving away too many state secrets if I said that commitment levels are not all they might be on those occasions. That probably explains why A teams usually do so well on tour – England A included. But on this occasion, I could have done with the game. I'd only bowled 24 overs against Hampshire and felt I needed another match under my belt and a decent bowl. It was not to be. The stop-go season continued. I had to wait another week for the National League game against Worcester (another poor performance from Lancashire, another defeat) and then the NatWest Trophy third round tie against Lincolnshire before I could get some serious bowling under my belt.

Lincolnshire at Cleethorpes. And to think it could have been a midweek trip to Amsterdam! When the draw was made, it was going to be either Cheshire, Lincolnshire or Holland for our first game in the competition once the preliminary rounds were out of the way. Amsterdam beckoned. The Dutch beat Cheshire in the first round, so it was wait-and-see time until they played Lincolnshire. Secret plans were made in anticipation of Lancashire's début on Dutch soil. There was even talk of being able to get hold of tickets for a Euro 2000 match. Tourist guides to Amsterdam started appearing in the dressing-room. Then Lincolnshire dumped Holland in the second round and it was Cleethorpes instead. Can't win 'em all!

I'd never actually been to Cleethorpes, let alone played cricket there. It was something of an unknown quantity for everyone. You always back yourselves against a Minor County in the early rounds, but funny things can happen and it's good to get a look at the wicket and a feel of the ground. As it happened, though, Cleethorpes provided us with a belter of a track and played into our hands. The better the pitch, the more it will suit the first-class county. And so it proved. One or two of their boys told me afterwards they had been disappointed to only make 180-odd. They felt they could have pushed it towards the 230 mark. But it wouldn't have mattered either way, because Athers and Ganguly went out and filled their boots.

It was Ravi's first really big one, and he needed it. He played like the whole world knew he could play and you could sense how relieved he was afterwards. It's taken him a while to settle into the rigours of county cricket and I don't think the weather has helped. But the signs are that he's coming to terms with what's involved and what's expected of him. He's knuckled down. After not having the best of starts, I can see him building on this and making a stack of runs.

Lincolnshire or not, though, it was an important win for us. With our one-day form, the last thing we needed was a scare against a Minor County. The win set us up for a quarter-final against Essex at Old Trafford and a chance to really get our act together. When you hit a sticky patch in one-day cricket, you have to go back to basics: do the simple things and do them properly, and build from there.

Which is exactly what I was planning to do when my calf went twang in the game against Northants. After that, the season I was gradually starting to re-build after my Mum's illness suddenly went pear-shaped again. I had to accept that I wasn't going to be around for a while. The first game I would be missing was a day-nighter against Yorkshire Phoenix at Old Trafford, followed by the first Roses Match of the season. When will it all end?

To be quite honest, I would have been glad to have kept my head down and stayed away for the Yorkshire Phoenix match. I knew there would be a big crowd and I didn't really fancy talking about my injury instead of dismantling the Yorkshire batting order. But during a Benefit year there are times when you need to see and be seen and, injured or not, this was obviously going to be a perfect chance to get out and say hello to people, introduce myself in the hospitality boxes and chat to a few fans as well. Did I say a few? I lost count of the number of people who came up as I wandered round and wished me well.

'How you doing, Oscar?'

'Get yourself fit, Bully lad. We need you back in the side.'

'Hope the Benefit goes well, Ian.'

'We wouldn't be getting stuffed like this if you were out there!'

It was non-stop, all round the ground. I'd be chatting to someone from the Benefit committee, who would introduce me to a couple of his mates. They would have pals of their own who'd always wanted to meet Oscar, and so on. I spent the whole of Yorkshire's 45-over innings wandering around, talking to people – mostly people I'd never met before. It brought it home to me how much the fans care about Lancashire cricket, and I suppose how much they think of me and the contribution I have made. You can't help feeling humble when you get a reaction like that. There are quite a few players who find it hard to get involved with supporters, but I've never really had a problem, although it isn't always easy to make conversation with a complete stranger. But I'm sure they feel the same way, too. The trouble is that they see Ian Austin, professional cricketer, rather than Ian Austin, human being. They don't know whether to talk cricket or not. If not, what do they talk about? And I don't know whether they'll think I'm arrogant if I talk about the game, or ignorant if I never mention the subject.

I've always believed talking to the fans is a big part of the job. It can be a bit of a bind, to put it mildly, when you've had a bloody awful day and someone collars you as you're loading the car. All you want to do is get home for a bite to eat, and here's this chap wanting go through the day's play in intimate detail or recall that day back at Worcester in 1987 when I bowled Botham. But I always give them a few minutes. At the end of the day these people help to pay your wages, so if you can't give them something back it's a poor do. I don't think I've ever knowingly bombed someone out, provided they haven't been downright rude to me in the first place. When I'm playing for Lancashire I'm on duty, and talking to supporters about cricket is part and parcel of each day. These days, I've been around long enough to know quite a few of the members' faces and to recognise a lot of the regular supporters. I also meet people at all sorts of functions: golf days and so on. But while I have a great memory for faces I can't remember names from one day to the next. It gets a bit embarrassing when all I can do is call people Pal or Mate. I don't suppose they mind, though.

In the end it turned out to be a good night, apart from Yorkshire's performance out in the middle. I was the lucky one. I spent most of the time walking around behind the scenes and missed some pretty grim action for the Red Rose. Another National League defeat, this time by 69 runs. Not exactly a perfect way to end the month.

June was a month when I thought I could get back on track. Instead I was faced with the bleak fact that no one had any real idea about when I would be able to play cricket again, so it was a month of few highlights, although I was grateful for the chance to remind myself how much Lancashire cricket means to so many people. And I also had an opportunity to go back to where it all began: Haslingden CC.

That was on 10 June, in a Lancashire League Worsley Cup quarter-final against Lowerhouse. At the time, I needed all the cricket I could get. So when Ernie Taylor, the Haslingden chairman, gave me a call and asked if I would be available for a couple of games, I was more than happy to say yes. Paul Strang, their 2000 pro, had been called up by Zimbabwe for the one-day series against England and the West Indies and Haslingden would need deputies for about six weeks. They had promised to stage a Benefit match for me later on in the season, so I was only sorry I couldn't offer to make it a more permanent arrangement. But I had commitments at Lancashire, and I also had one or two Benefit functions on the horizon. Part of the pro's job in the Lancashire League is to stay behind in the bar afterwards and have a drink with members, teammates and the opposition, and I didn't want to be packing my bags after the close and dashing off to a Benefit do. I was happy enough to fit in on a one-off basis, though.

It was great to be back. I still have a lot of old mates playing for the club or connected to it in some way or another. We beat Lowerhouse fairly easily and I enjoyed every minute – apart from hitting myself on the head with my bat after an elaborate follow through. I made some runs and picked up a wicket or two, and I can vaguely remember leaving the ground afterwards!

I was pencilled in for the semi against East Lancashire as well, but then the injury struck and I had to pull out. Joe Scuderi took my place. Before joining Lancashire at the start of the 2000 season, Joe had been a front-line pro in the league for a long time, first with Nelson and then with Colne. He helped Haslingden into the final against Todmorden – the team I had faced in my very first Worsley Cup final way back in 1982. It's incredible how history repeats itself.

As June turned into July, though, there was no way of knowing whether I would be available for the final if required. In fact, there was no way of telling when I would be playing cricket again. For anyone, anywhere.

18 JULY

The nightmare goes on. Apart from a Benefit game at his home club, Haslingden, on 27 July, when he gingerly bowls a handful of overs, Austin does not make a single appearance at any game of cricket in the whole of the month – far and away his longest spell out of action. Even this most easy-going and jovial of men is finding it hard to keep up appearances.

At first it wasn't so bad. You look at the positive side, don't you? You think: well, I've missed the day-nighter with Yorkshire, I've missed the Roses Match at Old Trafford and I'm not going to be around for the NatWest quarter-final against Essex. But out for four or five weeks? You must be joking! The last time I hadn't held a bat for that long, I was still in nappies.

At first I was having treatment from Lawrie Brown every day and the calf was improving all the time. Within three days of picking up the injury, I was walking OK. I soon started a bit of easy jogging and then I was doing some light bowling in the nets. I was sure I would be back way ahead of schedule. But Lawrie kept warning me it could be four, five or six weeks; one or two of the lads who'd had similar injuries said it might be even longer. No chance! I was making great progress. At first . . .

But as soon as I started to put in that little bit extra, I felt a twinge. I'd give it ten or 15 minutes nice and easy in the nets and then press the accelerator for the last five – and the pain would be back again. So Lawrie told me to ease up again. One step forward, one step back. On

6 July, only about two weeks after the injury, we all reported to Old Trafford in the morning. After a workout, the first team would be setting off for Derby for a four-day game, then going straight down to Taunton for a Championship match and a National League game. That was scheduled for Sunday 16 July. I reckoned that with ten days still to go, I could confidently target that one for my comeback, hopefully with a couple of Second XI one-day games in between.

That Wednesday morning, we had a middle practice. Pete Martin and me both joined in and it felt great right from the start. The ball was coming out really well. Chucky said I looked good, the best practice bowling he'd seen for a while. I had no problems at all, didn't feel a thing. I was flying. I was on the way back. I did 20 minutes, working up through the gears to more or less full pace. 20 minutes was the time limit, and those 20 minutes felt like 20 seconds so I thought I'd just have a few more. Everything felt so good, then bang! On the first ball of my extra stint, there was a searing pain in my right calf. I pulled up straight away and slumped on to the pitch. I could have cried. Oh no, not again. Lawrie came over: 'How is it, Bully?' He didn't need to ask. I didn't need to answer. I couldn't answer. He had a good look, I tried to walk a few paces and it felt a bit easier. Back into the dressing-room, shower, chat with Lol. He had a good look at the leg and was convinced I hadn't torn the muscle again. I was convinced I had – but he's the expert. He said the new injury was like knocking the scab off a wound. A torn muscle develops scar tissue and every now and then you damage the scar. That's what I'd done. One step forward, two steps back this time.

I got in the car and set off home. The rest of the lads left for Derby and Taunton. I watched them go, the outsider looking in. What had I done to deserve this? I'd never really been injured before in my life. How could I be starting now? And even though Lawrie said the muscle hadn't been torn again, I knew I was back on the treadmill. Treatment every day, a bit of light jogging, a bit of easy bowling. See how it goes, stop if it starts to hurt. If only I had a pound for every time I've heard those words . . .

The Second XI comeback targets came and went. First it was July 10 and a one-day game against Durham at Seaton Carew. The latest knockback put paid to that, and to the one-dayer against Yorkshire at Castleford the next day. After that, I was pencilled in for another one-day game against Worcester, this time nearer home at Radcliffe on July 13. Sorry, Oscar, you're not ready yet. Rest it up a while longer. Next target? Well, that National League game at Taunton on July 16 was clearly a non-starter now, but what about Leicester on Sunday 23 July? Perhaps you should give that one a miss, to be sure you're right for the NatWest quarter-final against Surrey at The Oval on July 26. We want you ready for that one.

In the end, I just ran out of time. Instead of being involved in a high-profile quarter-final, I was stuck at home in front of the box. Bloody hell, it isn't as if I didn't try hard enough. Baxenden CC is just round the corner from me and I popped up there a few times to test it out in the nets, sometimes with the rest of the Baxenden boys and sometimes on my own. Just me and a few cricket balls. But always, whenever I would try to accelerate, push myself a bit, nothing happened except that all-too-familiar twinge in the right calf. Time to pack up and go home.

Home? There were definitely times when I wasn't exactly a barrel of laughs for Alex and the kids. I've never been a man to take my work home; work is work, home is home. But this was different. It wasn't work, was it? I should have been out there playing cricket, helping the lads put together a successful run in all the competitions but instead of being involved, I was going nowhere. All I could do was sit on my backside and worry. When would I be back? Would I ever be back? You wouldn't believe how frustrating it was – far and away the most difficult time of my career. And inevitably there were times when I took it out on Alex, Victoria and Matthew. Once or twice, I just stuck Oscar the dog in the car, drove up on to the tops and took him for a long walk, just to relieve the tension, calm myself down. To clear my head rather than taking it out on the other three. It's not their fault, is it?

Alex and the kids are everything to me. Normally, it's a bit of a downer for them all when I put the gear in the car and set off down the motorway for an away trip but I bet they would have been glad to see the back of me while I was injured. I started getting angry about petty things that wouldn't normally bother me at all. The little ones didn't understand it, I could tell. They're only kids, aren't they? They want to play and mess about. But if it wasn't the right thing at the right time, their dad bit their heads off. It all added to the tension.

Thankfully, though, the boys managed OK without me in July. We finished the month in the top three in the Championship after beating Yorkshire, Derbyshire and Durham, and drawing down at Somerset and in the Roses Match at Headingley. The last day was washed out with us at 20 ahead with eight wickets in hand, and the Yorkies will no doubt try to tell you they had it won. Rubbish! A spectacular win at Surrey in the NatWest earned us a semi-final against Gloucester at Bristol in a couple of weeks, and great television coverage from The Oval!

I don't normally enjoy sitting in front of the telly, but I had to make an exception when Andrew Flintoff started to take the Surrey attack apart when we were chasing 211. He finished with 135 from 111 balls, with four sixes and 19 fours. We won by eight wickets. What a player! What an innings! It was the perfect retort to all the people who had been having a go at him because of his weight, an answer to the jibes that he lacks the commitment to go all the way for England. Hopefully, this innings would silence the knockers and people would shut up about his weight and concentrate on his cricket instead.

The result didn't come as a surprise to anyone inside the dressing-room, because we've always known what Flinty is capable of and he's performed like that once or twice before. Unfortunately, he doesn't do it on a regular basis. But give him a chance – he's only 22, after all. There are bound to be times when he just isn't going to cover himself in glory. That's the way he plays, and with experience he'll smooth out the rough edges, provided he's allowed to concentrate on what he does best – playing cricket.

At the end of the day, Flinty should be judged on his performances on the cricket field. If they are not up to scratch, find the answer in his cricket, not his eating habits. He doesn't keep getting out because he's overweight, he gets out because there are flaws in his technique which need ironing out. He needs patience and sympathetic handling, not headlines in the tabloid press accusing him of being a fatty. That was the last thing Flinty needed as he tried to come to terms with international cricket. If the authorities had a problem, they should have taken him to one side, talked it through with him and said: 'Right, this is where we're going, this is what you need to do. It's up to you to come up with the goods. We've put our cards on the table . . . now it's your turn. If you don't respond, we'll tell the press what's happening.' Instead, as I understand it, Flinty found himself on the back pages before he really knew there was a problem. The situation could have been handled better.

OK, so Flinty could probably do with losing a few pounds here and there; so could most people. But he's a big, strong lad and there's no guarantee that he would be a better cricketer if he lost weight. In fact, from personal experience I'm pretty sure he wouldn't. I also know that he's immensely talented and if we encourage him to do what he does best, cricket, then England and Lancashire will benefit. If we continue to get on his back, though, he'll become confused and worried, and will end up under-performing. I'm certain that has been part of his problem this season.

These days, the finger is always going to be pointed at players who enjoy a bite to eat, who carry a bit of extra weight or who like a couple of beers at the end of the day. People like me and Flinty, I suppose. But in the past, nobody worried when Fred Trueman and Brian Statham had a few pints in the evening, did they? And I'm reliably informed they weren't bad players. Even when I first started, you could have a beer with your lunch at Lord's. Not any more. Now, players who don't conform are regarded as suspect. I just hope it all works out for Flinty, because if ability were all that counted, he'd be in there every time.

I can sympathise with him, because I've been down the same path myself. In my younger days, people used to talk about me being a potential Test player – if only I'd lose a bit of weight. I chose to ignore that kind of remark and get on with my game, and I've never let anybody down. Until this calf injury, I've never had any long-term fitness problems. As I said right at the start of this book, I'm sure I would have played for England much earlier if people had looked at my figures and not my waistline. It won't be easy for Andrew, though, because in this day and age, if you don't look right people seem to think you can't play right either. And that's nonsense.

Flinty's first priority must be to cure the back problem that has bothered him for the last couple of seasons. In fact, it's been a problem for him since he was 12 or 13. He's had all sorts of different treatments, and hopefully they'll get to the source of the problem eventually. If that means he has to give up bowling, so be it – he's easily good enough to go all the way as a batter. The trouble is, Flinty will get bored out of his mind if he can only bat. He's the kind of person who wants to be in the game all the time, batting, bowling or fielding.

He's been on the staff since he was 15, and at first he was a very quiet, shy lad. On his first pre-season tour he wouldn't touch a drop of the hard stuff, but that didn't stop him picking up a few 'fines' for various misdemeanours inside and outside the dressing-room from the Fines Committee, though. It's one of our tour rituals: all the players come under scrutiny from the Fines Committee and on the last night, debts have to be paid in full. That means downing a drink in one go, or skulling it, as we say. We have a chairman who keeps an eye on offenders throughout the tour; a Fines Master, who decides the appropriate penalty; and a Weights and Measures Inspector, who's there to make sure all the drink has been consumed, or a reasonable effort to do so made. If not, you have to start again.

As Flinty wasn't a drinker on his first trip, we ordered in a crate of coke just for him. His list of offences ran and ran. He downed his first bottle, only to be recalled because he'd left a load of froth in the bottom. Same again second time round. He was all right with the third and was allowed to sit down. But two minutes later, he was called up for another *faux pas* committed in the early stages of the tour. He struggled desperately and eventually had to bale out on his fifth bottle. The following year, he'd learned his lesson and had progressed to lager. Flinty has come full circle now. No more Mr Shy Boy. He's everywhere – just like his kit. Flinty is even more untidy than Athers. He's a good lad, though, and potentially a great cricketer. He's a natural, and throughout his career he's found the game very easy. It was inevitable that England would come calling and I just hope he can go on and fulfil all that potential. If not, he'll have to settle for a place in the Fatties XI alongside me and a few other so-called heavyweights.

Actually, I prefer to see them as cricketing heavyweights. The side featured in a press article soon after Flinty had been pilloried for his weight and the name of Ian Austin was up there in lights, along with some of the greatest players in the history of the game: men like W.G. Grace, Ian Botham, Colin Cowdrey, Shane Warne, Colin Milburn, Mike Gatting, David Boon and Rod Marsh. Not the worst of sides, by any means. I certainly had no worries about being selected alongside those boys. So if you ever feel a bit concerned about your England prospects, Andrew, give us a call. We'll find you a place.

Another month has gone by. Today is 31 July. Monday. It's raining. The Roses Match at Headingley has been abandoned. Alex, Victoria and Matthew have gone off to Lanzarote for a holiday. I had a run-out in a Benefit game at Haslingden on Thursday and it went OK. No searing pain, no reaction the next morning. But it was very gentle stuff. I should have been playing in a friendly game at Wigan today to give the leg another workout, push it a bit more, but when I arrived the covers were floating around on the square. Game off. And so it goes on.

But tomorrow is another month. We've a spell of five one-day games in nine days coming up and I want to be involved; I want to play in them all.

I've had enough of the frustration, I've had enough of sitting around waiting for the thing to get better. It's time I played some cricket again.

Tomorrow, England and the West Indies will be at Old Trafford for two days' preparation before the third Test, which starts on Thursday. I'm hoping to go along and have a bowl at the England players in the nets. I'm looking forward to it. I've a gut feeling that the worst is over, and this will be a good test. It will be good to see the England boys again – and the West Indians. I know their coach, Roger Harper, well and we'll have a chat. I'll have a word with Jimmy Adams, too. Another good lad. And in the evening, there's a big Benefit dinner in the Old Trafford Indoor School with nearly 700 guests. Mike King and Dermot Reeve are speaking and hopefully, a good night will be had by all.

Who knows, before long I might even be able to play a game of cricket. I have had offers. As I watched the rain coming down yesterday, the fax machine rumbled into life. It was a message from the Prison Service, asking if I would be interested in playing a friendly next weekend. They didn't say whose side I'd be on, though!

19
AUGUST

At last, things are looking up. Austin finally regains his fitness and returns to the Lancashire side for five one-day matches that will be pivotal to how the season will turn out. But if Austin's problems off the field have finally eased, his return to active service does not mean that life out in the middle is going to be a picnic. Not by any stretch of the imagination.

With the Lancashire lads away in London for the Championship match against Surrey, Lawrie and Bob told me to work on my own, keep in touch, report on my progress and if everything went OK, to make myself available for the National League game against Sussex at Hove on Monday, 7 August, two days after the end of the four-day match at The Oval.

I was due down at Old Trafford on the first of August anyway, for a light workout and to see John Cotton, my Benefit chairman, about the do that night. I took time out to have a word with Duncan Fletcher, the England coach, and he was more than happy for me to join in their workout as a net bowler. I told him I would only be able to manage 20 minutes or so. No problem. It went well. There was no reaction from my leg during the session, and this time I didn't push it any further. I asked Duncan if I could have another bowl the next day, when the boys were practising in the morning. I was on the ground anyway, as I'd stayed in the Old Trafford Lodge after the Benefit night. I managed another 20 minutes before a Manchester shower forced us to abandon the session. Once again, I came through without any problems.

But I knew that the real test was still ahead of me. I'd been this far down the road before, only to break down when I stepped on the gas. Sooner or later, I was going to have to give it that final push. The first opportunity came on Test match Thursday. Obviously I couldn't practice at Old Trafford, so I asked the Haslingden boys if I could join in their evening session. They were due to play in the Worsley Cup final against Todmorden three days later, and were delighted to have an extra net bowler! I had no problems with it – all I was interested in was proving my fitness and it didn't matter whether I was bowling against England players before a Test match or league cricketers at their evening nets. I've always taken people exactly as I find them and I like to think they respond in the same way to me. Haslingden was where I learned my cricket and as far as I was concerned, it was perfectly natural for me to go back there when I needed an extra workout.

As it happened, it was still a bit wet under foot and I didn't feel like pushing too hard, so it turned out to be another gentle workout followed by some fielding practice, which involved running, some stop-start and a few games. Again, everything felt fine but I still hadn't really given it a go and I knew I couldn't ring Bob down at The Oval until I'd come through that barrier.

On the Friday, I got in the car and drove up to Baxenden CC. There was no one else around. I loosened up, bowled a few gentle overs, did some 40-yard shuttle runs. Built up the confidence. But I still had to face the big test. I was the only person who would know whether I was fit or not, so I went into the nets again and did half a dozen deliveries at full stretch. I waited for the reaction, for the searing pain. It never came. I drove home, picked up the phone, rang Bob and made myself available for Monday. He told me to drive down to Brighton on Sunday afternoon and link up with the rest of the team at their hotel. I was back in the frame. At two o' clock on Sunday I packed my bags, chucked all my gear in the car and hit the road. I arrived around seven p.m., had a bite to eat and an early night. Monday morning I went for a stroll around the town and a light lunch. Then it was action stations.

The boys had just finished eight days of Championship cricket, a drawn game against Yorkshire at Headingley and a heavy defeat by Surrey in that vital game at The Oval. They'd had just one day off in between the two four-dayers to travel down to London. Now it was the turn of the one-day circus. A Sunday off in Brighton while I was driving down then, in the space of eight days, five games that would almost certainly decide our fate for the season in limited overs cricket.

The sequence of games was this: Monday night, Sussex Sharks at Hove, National League; Wednesday night, Yorkshire Phoenix at Headingley, National League; Friday, Gloucester Gladiators at Old Trafford, National League; Sunday, Gloucestershire at Bristol, NatWest Trophy semi-final; Tuesday night, Kent Spitfires at Old Trafford, National League. Five games, three days' travelling, one day off. Nine days in the life of the English County pro.

We had to win two of the four National League games in order to move away from the foot of the table and give ourselves a reasonable chance of avoiding relegation. Ever the optimist, I reckoned that if we won all four, we might just be back in with a shout for the title. And the importance of the semi-final spoke for itself.

SUSSEX SHARKS, 7 AUGUST

I bowled in the nets before the game and had a bit of fielding practice. No worries there, but you can get away with a lot in the nets. The crunch comes out in the middle. There's no hiding place out there. John threw me the new ball. Was I nervous? No. Wary? Yes. Very. Chris Adams was the batter: a dangerous opponent. Dot ball, dot ball, next one just outside off stump, a slash, an edge, Flinty at slip, thank you very much!

I bowled seven overs with the new cherry and finished with one for 14. I was more than happy with that. Then I bowled at the death after a rain interruption. The outfield was wet and the ball was like a bar of bloody soap. It was a white-knuckle job keeping hold of it in the run-up. We were no-balled twice for deliveries above waist height, but there wasn't anything we could do about it. Slower balls ended up as beamers; the ball just flew out. Sussex did well at the end – they had a bit of luck with balls that went up in the air but didn't go to hand. And to be fair, we didn't bowl as well as we might have done.

Because of the interruption, Duckworth-Lewis was brought in and even though Sussex had totalled 213 for six from 41 overs, our revised target was 220 from the same number. Work that one out if you can! But it was a decent deck, and we should have got them with a bit to spare.

We lost a couple of early wickets, it started to rain, we stayed on. We pushed the ball around when we should have been getting on with it, fell behind the rate, lost more wickets and ended up chasing eight or nine an over. We finished 28 runs short. It never really happened for us. But then it never does when you're not playing well.

YORKSHIRE PHOENIX, 9 AUGUST

There are some games you wish had never happened. This was one of them. It was a game to forget, a game when absolutely everything went wrong. A game to put behind us as quickly as possible.

It didn't feel right from the beginning. One or two of the Yorkshire lads had a word with me when I was signing autographs in the players' tunnel before the start. Darren Lehmann, their overseas man, who was captain because David Byas was injured, gave me a big bear hug. A good man. He was in the Aussie squad in the Hong Kong Sixes three years ago. 'How's it going, Bully!' It was going well then. But that was 25 minutes before the start of the game.

We didn't bat well. Every time we hit it up in the air it went to hand. We missed too many straight ones, and had two silly run-outs. Yorkshire were up for it, and once they'd got hold of us they weren't going to let go. Darren Gough, Matthew Hoggard and Craig White kept coming at us hard and we just folded like a pack of cards. Sixty-eight all out, our second-lowest score in the competition. You can't defend a total like that. All you can do is put the close fielders in, attack them and hope for a couple of very early breaks – and a few miracles.

We got the early break when Vic Craven chipped me to mid-wicket, but the good times ended there. That was the signal for Mr Lehmann to stride to the crease. This time there were no friendly bear hugs, no 'How's it going, Bully!' He went straight for the jugular. Lehmann knew — we all knew – that with a decent batting line-up to follow, he could afford to come out and blaze away. We had two slips and a gully up for the catch, the wicket wasn't doing a lot and after sizing things up for a couple of overs, he set about us. With close fielders in, there were plenty of gaps and Lehmann found them. Mainly off my bowling. I copped the brunt of it in the shape of 39 runs in 6.5 overs. Halfway through, John asked me how I felt. I told him I'd carry on and that's what he wanted, too. He said it would do me good to bowl a few overs after the lay-off. So I bowled, Lehmann attacked and after 13.5 overs we were finished.

I would have liked a couple of scouts out on the legside boundary because that would probably have prolonged it a bit, made him change his plan and work for the runs, give us all a bit more time out in the

BULLY FOR YOU, OSCAR 183

middle. But John stuck with the close catchers and Lehmann kept hitting over the top.

Back in the dressing-room at 7.20 p.m., we were shellshocked: desperately disappointed about our innings and even more disappointed about the way their innings went. Morose and despondent. John had a bit of a chat, told us there was nothing we could do about it now. 'Go home, think about what's happened, why it happened, what we could have done different. Think about your own contribution, how much more you could have done. Come back Friday and we'll start all over again.'

My thoughts entirely. After a performance and a result like that, you don't need anyone telling you how much you've let yourselves and the supporters down. You know only too well. I sat quietly in the dressing-room for 20 minutes, thinking about what had gone wrong. How else I could have played it. But let's be honest, when you go out to bowl with 68 on the board and 45 overs to go, there's not a lot you can do. That's not an excuse; it's a fact. Unless you're playing on a minefield, you're going to lose. And this was a decent enough pitch. However well you bowl, you only need a player to come in, swing the bat, hit a quick 20 or 30 and that's it, done and dusted. I would have liked to make them work more for their runs, try and keep them to a run a ball, eke the game out for longer. But the bottom line is that we were awful and we got what we deserved.

I packed my bag and drove home. I arrived at about nine o'clock, something like three-and-a-half hours ahead of schedule. Alex had been watching it on the box. We looked at one another, I shrugged and we exchanged rueful grins. What else could we do? Here I was, back home in Baxenden putting the kettle on, when by rights I should have been getting stuck into the top of the Yorkshire batting order. Certainly a one-off.

I've never sat around moping after a defeat. If you let it get to you like that, you might as well write out your letter of resignation and pack it in there and then. Defeat hurts, but you have to react to it by coming out stronger next time, by bouncing back, not by wallowing in a pit of despair – but I was worried about the feel of the dressing-room. I'd been out of the side for a long time. I had been on the outside and not closely involved, so until now I hadn't seen for myself how the boys were responding to these setbacks in the National League. I could sense the spirit wasn't good. It never is when a side is on a losing streak, of course, but after two games back, I felt the spark was missing.

At that stage, I believed we had the ability to get out of trouble. But with only six more games to play, time was running out. We needed to start winning. And fast.

GLOUCESTER GLADIATORS, 11 AUGUST

Back in business! We reported early, had a spot of lunch, a net and a quick chat. John, Bob and Neil Fairbrother all said their bit: the next three games would make or break our season in one-day cricket. There were to be no more slip-ups, 100 per cent concentration. Then we had a fielding workout that was as intense as anything I can remember.

Gloucester won the toss and decided to bat. We reduced them to 28 for six. It was a decent wicket. Jack Russell stuck around for a while and they finished up with 137 for nine from their 45 overs, but the damage had been done. We had built a winning position. I bowled my nine overs straight through at the beginning and took four for 14. Highly delighted. Then Ravi went out and played an innings of the highest class. He hit a century, John took the chance to have a bit of batting practice and it was all over with 13 overs left. Four points, a big victory over our NatWest semi-final opponents and just the pick-up we needed after Headingley.

GLOUCESTERSHIRE, 13 AND 14 AUGUST

Goodbye Lord's for another year: Gloucestershire 248 for seven, Lancashire 150. A desperately poor performance. On the coach home, Warren commented that this had to be about as low as it gets. I agreed. In the past, we've always been able to get over a defeat pretty quickly; cricket has never been a matter of life and death. But this one really hurt. Losing a semi-final is bad enough; not competing is a different matter altogether. And let's face it, Gloucester hardly knew they'd been in a game.

The whole weekend started badly with a five-hour journey on the Saturday and massive hold-ups around Bristol, making us late for our evening workout at the ground. On Sunday morning, though, the adrenaline was flowing. We had a good net and had just started fielding practice when it started to rain. It didn't stop all day.

I felt desperately sorry for our supporters. They'd driven down to Bristol that morning for our second semi-final of the season against Gloucester and, like the players, all they could do was stand around and watch the rain. There was never any real prospect of play, so why they didn't call it off early and put us all out of our misery I'll never know. It was probably because the game was due to be televised. It strikes me that television calls the shots these days. There was a time when both semi-finals were played on the same day and one of them chosen for TV. Not any more. So while Warwickshire and Hampshire played their semi-final in uninterrupted sunshine on the Saturday, Gloucestershire and Lancashire were kicking their heels 24 hours later.

What do players do in these situations? Play cards, read the papers, pop outside every now and then to have a chat with the punters, make a few calls, anything to pass a few minutes. Long before the game was officially called off, most of our supporters had packed up and gone home. There was no way they could afford to stay overnight in Bristol, let alone take a day off work. If only the game had been played on the Saturday instead! We headed back to the hotel, had a bite to eat, checked the weather forecast and had another early night.

Monday was also a huge anti-climax – a small crowd and a dire performance. To cap it all, the television people who dictated when the game had to take place didn't cover the match live.

We were all convinced Kim Barnett had been caught behind by Chucky in Glenn Chapple's opening over. The close fielders said the ball nicked the toe end of his bat as he tried to pull it out of the way of a wide delivery. But Alan Whitehead said not out and things went downhill from there. I've no complaints about Kim staying put, even though I'm one of the last surviving members of an endangered species otherwise known as 'batsmen who walk'. I was brought up to believe that cricket is an honest game so if I nick it, I go, and down the years I've had plenty of umpires who've thanked me for setting off and making their job easier. Thanks from the umpires . . . bollockings from the captain! These days, virtually all players stay put and leave it to the umpire. They say it's swings and roundabouts: some you win, some you lose. Fair enough – but if you choose not to walk, it's no good complaining when the other side play it the same way.

It's the same with appeals. I only go up if I genuinely believe the batsman is out. Again, it's the way I was taught to play the game. But more and more, players are appealing when they know damn well the batter isn't out. Gamesmanship? More like cheating, in my book, just like batsmen who try to con umpires by rubbing their arm or shoulder when they know they've hit the ball, or batsmen who say they stood their ground because they weren't sure whether or not they'd hit the ball. Not sure? You must be joking! If you don't know whether you hit the ball or not, you shouldn't be playing first-class cricket. Or any class of cricket, for that matter.

Anyway, Kim stayed. He made 80 and their total was arguably 20 or 30 too many. But we should have made a better fist of it. We lost early wickets as usual, lost two more with silly run outs and by the time I went out to bat, it was up to 10 or 12 an over. Digger was last man and we decided that we needed a bit of batting practice after hardly playing all summer. So we stuck around and put on 36 for the last wicket before Pete was stumped by Jack Russell. Alan West, our scorer, told us afterwards that we'd missed a new Lancashire last-wicket record in the competition by just one run. That just about said it all.

Two semi-finals at Bristol, two defeats. It doesn't get much worse than that.

KENT SPITFIRES, 15 AUGUST

They say that when you fall off a bike, the best thing to do is get straight back on. I'm not convinced of that. I'm certain most of the boys would have given anything for a break after the Gloucester game. We'd hit rock bottom. It was time to recharge our batteries. Given the choice, we would have opted for a day or two to come to terms with it and prepare for yet another big one. But we had no choice. Less than 24 hours after losing a semi-final at Bristol, we were back out against Kent on the same pitch as the game against Gloucester Gladiators the previous Friday. There the similarity ended.

The boys looked shot to pieces. I hadn't been around for most of the summer, so I could see what the rest of the players, apart from Digger who had also spent most of the summer on the sidelines, couldn't see for themselves. They were tired, they'd been on the road more or less non-stop for 18 days, they wanted a break. Above all, they'd lost three games out of four, one of them a semi-final. A winning side can run on adrenaline. They can hide the tiredness and the knocks behind the confidence that winning brings, and the lucky breaks go their way. But when you're losing, the confidence drains away, the banter dries up, the bickering starts. You begin to feel all those little niggles.

To make matters worse, when we arrived at Old Trafford to prepare for the Kent game, it was raining. Would we start or not? When the rain finally stopped and the mopping-up operations had been completed, there was only time for a 21-over game. To be honest, the pitch wasn't fit and in a perfect world, the game would never have started. But both teams were at the wrong end of the table, and two points were no use to either side. And, of course, the television cameras were there . . .

Inevitably, they focused on an empty players' balcony when Ganguly completed his half century. He was the only batsman who got a start and went on, but he also ran out Andrew Flintoff and Neil Fairbrother, who were not best pleased, to put it mildly. The players' reaction, or lack of it, to his 50 was picked up by the media who saw it as a deliberate snub to Ganguly after those run-outs. That was inevitable, I suppose, but I was in the dressing-room and I certainly didn't see it that way. Neither did Ravi when he came back in.

I'll talk about Ganguly and his contribution on and off the field later, but the absence of players applauding on the balcony was not designed to be a public snub to the overseas man. Nobody was out on the balcony in the first place. Two of the lads were having treatment and a couple more weren't around at all – we don't spend every minute of every game watching the action out in the middle, you know. If people had looked carefully, they would have spotted at least five Lancashire players applauding Ganguly's 50 from behind the dressing-room window.

Our no-show added fuel to the flames already aroused by the controversy of Ravi's blue boots. He had worn them when he went out to bat in the semi-final at Bristol and they attracted almost as much attention as the loose shot that cost him his wicket early in our innings. Almost straight away, rumours were flying around about dressing-room friction over Ravi's boots. I ask you! I can't think of one of the Lancashire players who gave a damn about the colour of his boots. He could have been wearing yellow boots with pink polka dots as far as we were concerned.

To a pro cricketer, it is results that matter, not the colour of a teammate's footwear. It just wasn't a serious issue among the players. If we'd been winning week in, week out, those boots would have become a talking point for all the right reasons and everyone would have had a good laugh about it. Instead we were playing badly, relegation was a very real threat and the sight of our overseas man wearing coloured shoes sparked a load of aggro from the fans. 'It's no wonder he doesn't get any runs wearing boots like that,' was a typical reaction from a lot of people. They wouldn't have been saying that if he'd scored 150 at Bristol and we'd been heading back to Lord's.

Irrespective of the colour of his boots, our total of 141 for three against Kent could and should have been more. After a rain break, they were set a revised target of 137 off 21 overs. For a while it looked as if we might make it and with five overs left, they still needed 40. Then Rahul Dravid, their Indian overseas player, and Martin McCague took 20 off an over from Joe Scuderi, Chris Schofield came in for some tap and it was all over with 13 balls to spare, which is a lot in such a short game.

So, another defeat. Three defeats out of four in the competition. That left us with away games against Worcester Royals and Gloucester Gladiators (not again!), and home matches against Somerset Sabres and Sussex Sharks.

We were under no illusions; we talked it through afterwards, and we all knew that relegation was now a real possibility. Realistically, we were going to need four wins to have any chance of staying in the top division. We accepted that we weren't playing well: as a professional, you can never kid yourselves on that score. But a few of the boys had watched the highlights of the semi-final when they got home from Bristol and said we looked like a side who'd run out of luck as well. I've mentioned before that winning teams – teams like Gloucester – get the breaks. The catches go to hand when they're fielding, the edges fly out of range when they're batting. The 50-50 decisions go their way.

We hadn't played well in four of our five one-day games in August, those five games that would mean so much to our season, but we didn't have any luck either. That's the name of the game, though – there's no point whinging about it. You've just got to get your head down and get stuck in.

After the Kent game I went into the Committee Room for a drink, as usual. There's an open invitation to players from both teams, and their wives and families, to get together for a chat amongst themselves or with members of the committee. I've always tried to make a point of turning up. I always thought I could hold my head up in there, win or lose, however I had performed. So it was bitterly disappointing that when Warren and I walked into the room, everybody seemed to discover they had matters of great interest to discuss among themselves. Either that, or they had suddenly spotted something hugely interesting going on outside which grabbed their undivided attention. In a word, we were frozen out.

It was a shock. And it hurt. I would be the first to admit that the team had played badly, and my own bowling was not up to par either, but after all I've done for Lancashire I deserved better, and so did Warren.

We had a drink and cleared off. As I walked away, I vowed never to set foot in that room again.

OK, so things had been going badly. It looked like we were going to be relegated. It would have been oh-so-easy to send a message in to Alex asking her to meet us in the car park instead. But no – we'd been going in there throughout our careers and we weren't going to change because our team was in the middle of a bad run. I expected other people to respond in the same way, but it didn't happen.

I raised the subject with Jack Simmons a couple of days later. Me and Jack go back a long way, so I've always been able to talk to him as a pal and a former teammate rather than as the Cricket Chairman. I told him I felt that we'd been snubbed. He said I was over-reacting, that the committee members felt awkward and just didn't know what to say after so many poor results. If that was their excuse, so be it, but it didn't wash with me. And it never will.

There was another knock-back waiting for me when I arrived at the ground to warm up for the Championship match against Kent less than 36 hours after the day-night defeat. A big knock-back. I wasn't even in the squad. I had assumed, wrongly as it turned out, that I would be involved now that I was fit again. I had also assumed, again wrongly, that if I wasn't required somebody would have told me. So I reported for duty as usual and did all the pre-match build-up. Why not? The last time I had been fit for a Championship game was way back in the first week of June for the match against Hampshire at Liverpool. I'd done OK in that game, but because of my injury the Kent game was the first time I'd been available to play Championship cricket since then. So I turned up.

As we left the field after the warm-up at about 10.20 a.m., I bumped into Matthew Fleming, the Kent captain, who was unfit to play. He said he was glad to see I was 100 per cent fit again and asked if I'd be playing. All I could do was shrug and say: 'I don't really know. Nobody's told me yet.'

I went into the physio's room for a chat with Lawrie Brown. John Crawley was already in there, but again nothing was said. By that time it was pretty obvious I wasn't going to be involved, and apparently John had earlier asked Lawrie why I was at the ground. He wanted to know if it was some kind of fitness test or if I was having an extra net. Far from it. All I wanted to do was play cricket for Lancashire – not an unreasonable wish, after missing so many games. Instead, I was left hanging around like a spare part and after the season I had been through on and off the field, that was one indignity I could have done without.

I wasn't chosen for the game at Leicester the following week either, but at least this time I knew what to expect. Instead, I played for the Second XI against Warwickshire at Old Trafford. Funnily enough, my last game for the seconds had been against Warwickshire, too, at Stratford-upon-Avon last year, when it was a straight choice between Twelfth Man duties against Surrey at The Oval or a run-out with the Second XI.

This time it was a good game of cricket which went the distance. We lost by 12 runs. I was run out by a young trialist for 30-odd in the first innings. Done like a kipper. He was sick about it afterwards but I told him it wasn't the end of the world and to learn from his mistake – running out an experienced player when there's an extra bonus point 12 runs away isn't a good idea. Then I made a 50 second dig, but got out after taking us from 50 for five to within touching distance of our target of 220.

Before the game, I knew I needed to do some serious bowling so I was determined to get nearly 40 overs under my belt. I did. But it was weird; after playing so much one-day cricket, I was ready to come off after five or six overs before bowling my last three later on. Instead, I took the new ball and bowled 11 overs on the bounce. I also had to try to re-adjust to playing a longer innings, to convince myself that it didn't matter if I pushed a couple of overs straight back to the bowler. Batting down the order in one-day stuff, you're either trying to get on with it straight away or looking to steer the side out of trouble. It was a bit of a culture shock to be going into bat in the middle of the order knowing I could hang around for a whole day if I wanted. I kept telling myself: 'Chill out, relax. Enjoy it.' In the end, I did.

We finished the month with a cracking Benefit do down at Bishop's Stortford, a club that supports the Lancashire beneficiary year in and year out. It was their 175th anniversary and the start of a new millennium as well as my Benefit year, so they wanted to lay on something a bit special. They settled on a golf day, a dinner and a six-a-side cricket tournament. No problem. As it was on their doorstep, six Essex players agreed to come along for the golf, along with a few from Lancashire and one or two assorted celebrities. Bob Simpson said he would speak at the dinner.

With three days to go, I had a wake-up call from Bob Wilson, who was organising the event. The Essex players couldn't make it after all, four of the Lancashire lads needed a workout with the Second XI and Bob Simpson had too much on his plate at Old Trafford and wouldn't be able to speak at the dinner. Great! Bob Wilson and other members of my committee spent most of Bank Holiday Monday on the phone, trying to cajole people into playing in the golf match. In the end, we made it by the skin of our teeth. But it was a close one, and we still needed a speaker for the dinner.

Enter Mike Atherton. He was down in London preparing for the final Test against the West Indies at The Oval. England were due to net on Tuesday afternoon and when Athers heard about the problem, he offered to help me out. He drove up from London after nets, sat at the top table, made his speech and dashed away at 10.30 p.m. to beat the curfew at the team hotel. What could I say, except thanks, pal? No one was more delighted than me when Athers lifted the Man of the Match award after England beat the Windies for the first time in a series since 1969.

20
SEPTEMBER

Austin wrote earlier that at the start of a new season, the aim is to win every game, every trophy. It doesn't work out like that, of course. As the final month of the 2000 season began, those lofty targets had long since disappeared. Beaten by Gloucestershire in two one-day semi-finals, Lancashire began September with only the faintest hope of depriving Surrey of their second successive County Championship and only a marginally less remote chance of avoiding relegation from Division One of the National League. Surrey's first bonus point in Old Trafford's final four-day game of the season snuffed out the title dream for another year; a third one-day defeat at Bristol meant that survival in the higher division of the National League was no more than a notional possibility. For the first time since 1997, there is no silverware in the Old Trafford trophy cabinet.

To be brutally honest, if we'd been offered second place in the Championship at the start of the season we'd probably have taken it. Back in April, we sat down and talked our prospects through. With an overseas batter to strengthen a strong batting line-up, we had no worries about scoring runs. But without a Wasim or a Murali, would we be able to bowl sides out twice? That was the big area of concern. But what happened? We've performed well with the ball but not scored anything like enough runs. With the new bonus points system awarding five points for batting and only three for bowling, we have actually ended up picking up more bowling points. That says it all. The batting has been strong on paper but inconsistent out in the middle, where it matters.

Of course it has been frustrating to get so near but so far yet again, finishing runners-up for the third time in a row. But in fairness, Surrey were the strongest side in the competition. They have a world-class spinner in Saqlain Mushtaq, who's brought the best out of Ian Salisbury. Alex Tudor and Martin Bicknell have taken wickets consistently. Adam and Ben Hollioake could usually be relied on to chip in here and there – the most complete all-round attack in the game. The batting line-up is strong, even though Alec Stewart has been on England duty all season and Graham Thorpe has played in the later Tests. The best team won, and that's what the Championship is supposed to be all about.

How do we bridge the gap? Well, for starters there's talk of Murali, a world-class performer, coming back next season. He could be our missing link. He'll take a stack of wickets and with him around, we'll be able to get rid of nine, ten and Jack on a more regular basis. But even if Murali does return, the bottom line is that the batting will have to be more consistent.

In the one-day game, we have to accept that Gloucester are the new kings. With all three trophies in the bank, they have taken our crown. To rub it in, after they had beaten us in two knock-out semi-finals, we ended up handing them the National League title by beating Somerset in our last game but one. You can't argue against their record: five one-day trophies in two seasons. That's phenomenal. And do you know how they achieved their success? By copying Lancashire. They've been doing what made us successful for ten years.

When we were down at Bristol for the National League game at the start of the month I bumped into Jon Lewis, their pace bowler. Good mate, Lewie. He told me that at the start of last season, the Gloucester players had taken a long, hard look at their one-day performances and said: 'What's the secret? How can we become winners?' The unanimous verdict was to pick up on the formula that had earned Lancashire eight one-day trophies in the '90s. They looked at the Lancashire side, studied the role of each player and how those roles could be adapted to their own strengths, and now they are easily the most effective one-day unit in the game.

There's no secret formula to how they achieved that status. They are well-organised, they know their game plan, they stick to it. It's straightforward, it's simple, and I know from experience that if everyone in the side does his job, it works. They cut off boundaries, they pressure batsmen, they don't let them get off the hook with a couple of loose deliveries. They try to build their innings around one batsman who goes in at the start and reckons to be around at the death. The other players come in and make their runs around him. The proof of the pudding is in the results. They have adopted our methods and won trophies: we have slipped from our own high standards and missed out.

We did reach two semi-finals. But to be honest, we never really got our act together in the Benson & Hedges and had to get out of jail once or twice to go as far as we did. But it looked as if everything was coming together for the NatWest. We won at a canter against the Minor County and against Essex and then performed tremendously well to beat Surrey at The Oval. But in the semi-final, Gloucester strangled us again and it was 'goodnight Lancashire'.

The National League has been a disaster. For one reason or another, we'd only played a couple of games by early June and were already behind the pack. There was always a feeling of 'We only have to win our games in hand to be right up there. We can still win the league from here.' It was dangerous thinking. We were inconsistent, played really poorly once or twice and never made up the lost ground.

It would be easy to find ready-made excuses for our failure. We could look back and say that the team was without Pete Martin and me for a long spell in the middle of the season and our absence disrupted the whole bowling attack. For years, Digger and I have set the ball rolling. We've tried to keep it tight with the overseas man, Waz or Murali, as first change. Knowing one of them would be coming on when Digger and I had finished increased the pressure on the batters. Glenn Chapple, Mike Watkinson, Gary Yates and Andrew Flintoff helped to turn the screw. By and large, that's been the set-up. And it's been a winning pattern. But from an early stage in the 2000 season me and Digger were injured, there was no overseas bowler and Winker and Gary hardly played, so it was a whole new ball game, with people filling roles they weren't used to. When I returned at the start of August we should have been able to kick our way out of trouble, but by that time we weren't working as a unit; the spark was missing.

At the beginning of September we had four games left and realistically had to win at Worcester and Gloucester and beat Somerset and Sussex at Old Trafford to stand a chance. We beat Worcester on the last ball, lost heavily at Gloucester yet again and even though we performed up to standard at last and beat Somerset in another tight finish, other results had gone against us and barring miracles, it was all over.

It was massively disappointing. We've been used to success in one-day cricket and this year we never really had a serious sniff. Other counties will look and say: 'OK, you were poor in the National League but you reached two semi-finals and finished second in the Championship. We'll settle for a slice of that, thanks very much!' But it just isn't that easy. Expectations at Old Trafford are huge and we brace ourselves to be successful. Anything less than silverware in the trophy cabinet is regarded as a disaster. Those are the pressures we have lived with for years and usually we've come up with the goods. Not this time, though.

It hasn't helped that the overseas player this year has been a disappointment. Ganguly simply hasn't scored the weight of runs that either he or the rest of the team would have wanted. He was signed on the recommendation of Bob Simpson, who was convinced that Ravi would make stacks of runs. He was said to be desperate to come over to play for Lancashire and make his mark in the English game. Ravi has proved at the highest level that he can go and make very big scores in Test cricket and limited overs internationals, but it just didn't happen for him here. He hasn't really come up with the goods in the Championship, where he failed to make a hundred, a record that speaks for itself. Some of the ways he has got out have been pretty average, to say the least.

And while he's made runs in one-day cricket, he hasn't won us many matches, which is what the overseas player's role is all about. At the start of the season, we had a chat about what we were looking for in one-day games. We decided Ravi would open the batting with Athers when Mike was available. Ravi himself said that one of them should always be looking to bat more or less through an innings. But apart from the NatWest ties against Lincolnshire and Surrey and the National League games against Gloucester and Somerset late on, it hasn't really happened.

The bottom line for an overseas man is that he produces the goods out in the middle, but there's more to it than that. Just as a league pro is expected to play a full part off the field, so it's important that the overseas player becomes an integral part of the whole set-up and not just as a player. Unlike Waz and Murali, Danny Morrison and Steve

Elworthy, Ganguly never did that. He found it difficult from the start and always seemed to be complaining about the cold – but what did he expect? It was England, it was April and it was cold for us, too. The lads did their best to make him feel welcome, part of the dressing-room. They offered to take him out in the evenings but he didn't want to know. There's give and take in every situation, and the boys were happy to meet Ravi halfway, but he didn't seem inclined to do the same. He wanted to do his own thing. Before long, the feeling was that if he couldn't be bothered to make the effort, fair enough. Neither could we. There was never any huge bust-up. He just went his way and we went ours.

I would like to think that the Lancashire dressing-room is one of the easiest places in world cricket to fit into. There are no cliques, and it's always a load of laughs. Just ask Joe Scuderi. He moved here at the start of the season and slotted in right away. But it was different with Ganguly.

Don't get me wrong. Ravi hasn't been awkward and he hasn't caused any trouble, but he did choose to keep himself to himself and not socialise. On away trips, we always arrange to meet down in the bar at a certain time, to have a drink or just for a chat. In my experience, Ravi never joined us. At the start of the season his wife was over here too, so he travelled to long-distance away games with her rather than on the team coach. Again, that was his choice, and a team bus with a card school effing and jeffing at regular intervals isn't the place for a lady. But by not joining us, he missed out on a chance to get to know what made the lads tick.

It was so different with Murali. When he first arrived, I don't think he knew the King of Spades from the Three of Diamonds – or that's what he led us to believe, anyway! But after a few card sessions on the bus, he was a match for anyone. If you thought his bowling action was unique, you should have seen him shuffle a pack of cards! Whatever the situation, he just loved being one of the lads. It was as if he'd never been anywhere else. It was the same with Waz. In the evenings he would make a point of being one of the first to arrive in the lounge and would buy the boys a drink. Then he'd say: 'I know a great restaurant just round the corner. Anyone fancy a bite?'

Perhaps those two spoiled us. The dressing-room culture is an important part of the framework of a team. Everyone has to fit in, take the jokes on the chin and join in the banter. Ganguly didn't see it that way. In a way, I feel sorry for him. He missed out on something special. Maybe one day he'll look back on his time with Lancashire and wonder if he could have made more of it. Would it have been any different if he'd scored 1,500 runs and helped us win a Lord's Final? It may have been – we'll never know. But with hindsight, he simply wasn't the right man for the Lancashire dressing-room.

What about my own season? From a personal point of view, the Championship was a complete non-event. I had to miss out at the start because of off-the-field problems, but I thought I'd made a case when I came back against Hampshire at Liverpool in early June and we won inside two days. I performed reasonably well, and then I did my calf in. I was never in contention from then on. Worse than that, I haven't even been in the squad.

It's been very frustrating. And even more disappointing is the fact that I was never really given a reason why I wasn't involved. I have been told by various people that I wasn't rated fit enough for Championship cricket, but I never could understand that. Before and after the calf injury, I was fit for one-day cricket and fit to play in four-day Second XI matches. Against Warwickshire Seconds at the end of August, I bowled nearly 40 overs and batted for a reasonable time in both innings. At the time, I was also bowling well in the one-dayers, so I thought I had every chance of being in the squad for the Championship game against Somerset at the beginning of September.

I wasn't. And how did I discover that I wouldn't be involved? I was informed that the meeting with the Lancashire top brass to discuss my contract for 2001 was timed for 10.45 a.m. on the first day of the Somerset game. As play was due to start at 10.30 a.m., I didn't have to be Albert Einstein to work out that I hadn't been picked. I just wish someone on the management side could have found the time to take me to one side and explain exactly what was going on.

Despite all that, I feel I've done well in one-day cricket. I've scored some important runs and performed well with the ball. I bowled my nine overs in each of those three important games against Worcester, Gloucester and Somerset and came out with figures of two for 18, nought for 15 and two for 34. In the three big games against Gloucester, the two semi-finals and the National League crunch match, I bowled 28 overs for 69 runs.

These days, I know my own game, my strengths and weaknesses, the fields I want to set. I know the job that is expected of me. I like to think that I have gone out there and got on with it. I would never dream of turning round and saying: 'Well, I did my bit and it's not my fault that we didn't win anything.' This is a team game and every individual works within the team unit. We stand and fall as one. But I can look back on my one-day season and say that apart from one or two below-par performances, I have played my part. Down the years, I've learned what the game is all about. The will to win is still there.

I still enjoy every minute, and I like to think that shows through in the way I approach a game. I'll always have a word with an opponent or a laugh and a joke with the umpires, no matter how tense it is out there. The game against Somerset at the start of the month was a classic example. It was always going to go right down to the wire and when I came back for my final couple of overs at the end, it could easily have gone either way. Peter Willey was the umpire, and he knew what a sore point Gloucester's one-day success had become with everyone at Old Trafford.

'Oscar, do you realise that if Somerset don't get these runs, Gloucester will be champions?'

'Thanks, Will. That's just what I want to hear. Now, do you mind if we get on with the game, please?'

After the first delivery, Willey went down the wicket and made a point of marking out the front foot line with the edge of his boot.

'Come off it, Peter. You know me better than that. If I bowl a no-ball now, it'll be the first in three years.'

After the next ball, he went down the track and inspected where my foot had landed. It was right there in the safe zone as usual.

'You always were a boring bastard, Austin!'

It was a tense situation for both of us, but we could still find time for a laugh. Isn't that how the game should be played? Or are people like me and Will the last of the dinosaurs after all?

It has been reassuring to find that even though I haven't been involved in the Championship, the supporters have still been right behind me. Against Somerset, the adrenaline was really flowing throughout the side for just about the first time all season in the National League. Batting, bowling and fielding were spot on, and the fans were fired up, too. They gave me a tremendous reception whenever I came on to bowl. It meant a lot. It always will.

I like to think I've always given supporters value for money on and off the field. Before the Somerset game, I was asked to make a presentation in front of the pavilion to a junior side. As always my answer was: 'Of course, it's not a problem.' The same has always applied to autographs, pictures, supporters' functions. It's meant more to me than just part of the job.

At 34, I'm under no illusions that I'll be around for ever. That feeling was reinforced when I reported for my contract meeting with Jim Cumbes, Lancashire's chief executive, and committee man Paul Allott. I'd been hearing whispers for a while that for the 2001 season, I would be offered a one-day contract, but there had been nothing concrete. It wasn't up to me to go barging in and ask what plans Lancashire had for me. I was happy to wait for the official meeting, which was arranged for Friday 8 September. So it was disappointing, to put it mildly, when I discovered before the meeting that one or two reporters had been tipped off in advance that I would only be offered a one-day deal for 2001. Reporters never give their sources away, of course, but somebody, somewhere had been talking too much, because there was a story about my future in an edition of the *Manchester Evening News* which appeared on the streets at roughly the same time as I was due to hear what the County were prepared to offer me.

I left Cumbes and Allott in no doubt as to what I felt about that particular state of affairs . . . and then waited to hear my fate. The reports were spot on. The powers-that-be saw me purely as a one-day player. It was a blow and I told them that I didn't agree with their assessment, but I accept that times change and eventually every player has to face up to the fact that he is coming towards the end of his career.

In fairness, a one-day contract will have its advantages. At 34, I've seen it all and done most of it when it comes to life on the road. In ten seasons as a capped player, I've had more than my fair share of motorways, hotel rooms and restaurants. Eventually, there comes a time when even nights out with the boys lose their appeal. I've always been a bit of a home bird and time with the family has always been precious. It's not a lot of fun sitting in a hotel-room in Canterbury, knowing that 250 miles further north, one of the kids isn't feeling so good. And even home games can be wearing. For a four-day game, I've always left home around eight o' clock in the morning and arrived back after eight at night. I'll be tired, hungry and if things haven't gone well, a bit bad-tempered. The kids sometimes stay up to say goodnight, but then they will be tired too, and a bit past it themselves. Too often, it has ended in tears. So more quality time with Alex, Victoria and Matthew will be a big plus.

Even though I begged to differ with the club's assessment of my four-day qualities, no one tried to deny that I am still an effective one-day player. If I'm going to be able to concentrate purely on limited overs cricket, at least I will know exactly where I stand. I won't have to endure another season of wondering whether I'm still part of the Championship set-up or not.

I'll be 35 next May but if I'm only playing one-day cricket, I believe I could well extend my county career by at least a couple of seasons. On top of that, Lancashire have said they would have no worries about me fixing up to play a full season in the leagues, so that will be a chance to put down one or two markers for the future. To be quite honest, life after first-class cricket isn't something I've sat down and thought long and hard about – that's not my style. I've had one or two approaches from people who want me to be involved on the corporate side in some capacity, and I'll have a think about those over the winter.

No doubt a few people will think I'd be able to make a go of it as an umpire. No chance! I can live without one full day in the field, never mind four on the trot. And I have a nasty feeling that if anyone was to hit the pads after 6.30 p.m. when I was looking forward to a thirst-quenching pint, the finger might just be raised! I've a lot of time for umpires, always have had, but I won't be joining them, thanks very much!

I just want to play cricket for as long as I possibly can and to stay involved in the game at some level for even longer. I'll go on and play in the leagues as a professional, and hopefully I'll be able to put something back in the way of coaching and development work, try to encourage youngsters to take up the game and, just as importantly, stick with it. Whenever I speak to people involved with league clubs, they go on about the number of kids they have coming to junior nets every week. Youngsters aged between six and 14 are flocking in, it seems. But how many of them go on and play first-team cricket? The problem is that once they reach the age of 15 or 16, other attractions start to kick in, cricket is no longer cool and they drift away from the game. Take a look at just about any league side and it's made up of experienced players and just a couple of teenagers who are making their way.

That's the wrong way round. We've got to encourage young players to stay with the game and feel they are part of the team, not just chosen to make up the numbers. It's no good for an up-and-coming bowler if the professional bowls 25 overs at one end and two experienced amateurs share the rest of the bowling at the other. It's no good, either, if the pro opens the batting and the next four slots are taken up with older players with the kids down at eight, nine and ten. If a lad isn't going to bat or bowl why should he stick around, however talented he may be?

Things have got to change. We must keep the young players. If we don't, cricket as we know it will be dead and buried in 25 years' time. And if the name, experience, enthusiasm and know-how of Ian Austin can play any part in building a better future for Lancashire and for England, count me in!

EPILOGUE
THANKS FOR THE MEMORIES

On 14 September 2000, an auction was held in the Long Room at Old Trafford: the Ian Austin Benefit Auction. The catalogue listed almost 150 different lots and almost every one was a memento of my cricketing life with Haslingden, Lancashire, my two Australian clubs and, of course, England. Bats and balls, shirts and sweaters and all sorts of other items of cricket equipment, ties, books, autographs, pictures. Some were mine; others had been donated by teammates, opponents and friends.

Until my Benefit committee came up with the idea of staging on an auction, most of this memorabilia was stashed away at home in wardrobes, cupboards, drawers, cardboard boxes, carrier bags and old tea chests. I'd never considered getting rid of it; this was my cricketing history, every item had some kind of significance. Balls that had taken vital wickets, shirts and caps from the World Cup and from Lord's triumphs with Lancashire. My first Lancashire youth-team sweater, a Young England sweater, an MCC sweater. The red boots that I wore in the National League before the ECB stepped in with a ban, nine of my Lancashire tracksuit tops (all large or extra large!), a battered cricket coffin.

When the Benefit committee suggested an auction, my first reaction was to say no. I couldn't even contemplate letting it all go. Friends told me I must be mad to even consider it. But what the hell! It was only gathering dust and cluttering up the house. I never really looked at any of it from one year to the next. Far better for it all to belong to genuine collectors, or be somewhere on show for cricket enthusiasts to go and see. And the cash would boost the Benefit fund, of course.

I kept my medals and one or two other little items that Matthew and Victoria might decide they want to hang on to when they are a bit older and then I said to the committee: 'It's all yours!' They were hoping to beat the previous record for an auction of memorabilia, which apparently stood at around £6,000. It was a good night, and at first I thought I would have some regrets as the mementoes I'd collected over so many years went under the hammer. But no. The memories that really matter will always be there in my mind and no one can ever take them away. They're in my scrapbook collection, too. And now they're in the pages of this book.

For the most part, they have been happy memories for me. And, I hope, for you, too.

STATISTICS

I D AUSTIN – ONE DAY INTERNATIONAL CAREER RECORDS

BATTING

	M	I	NO	RUNS	HS	AVGE
v India	2	2	0	4	2	2.00
v Kenya	1	–	–	–	–	–
v Pakistan	1	1	0	1	1	1.00
v South Africa	2	1	0	10	10	10.00
v Sri Lanka	3	2	1	19	11*	19.00
Totals	9	6	1	34	13	6.80

BOWLING

	O	M	RUNS	WKTS	AVGE	BEST	4WI	ECON
v India	15	0	94	0	–	–	–	6.26
v Kenya	9.4	0	41	1	41.00	1.41	–	4.24
v Pakistan	8	0	21	0	–	–	–	2.62
v South Africa	19	0	94	1	94.00	1.41	–	4.94
v Sri Lanka	27.3	2	110	4	27.50		–	4.00
Totals	78.7	2	360	6	60.00	2.25	–	4.54

ONE DAY MATCHES FOR LANCASHIRE

BATTING

		M	INNS	NO	RUNS	HS	AVGE	50
Sunday Nat. League	Total	193	117	47	1177	48	16.81	–
Benson & Hedges	Total	64	41	12	668	80	23.03	2
NatWest trophy	Total	33	23	10	361	97	27.76	2

BOWLING

		OVERS	MDNS	RUNS	WKTS	AVGE	B/B
Sunday Nat League	Total	1281.4	73	5593	210	26.63	5–30
Benson & Hedges	Total	608.4	78	2276	80	28.45	4–8
NatWest Trophy	Total	355.3	58	1203	44	27.34	3–14

CAREER RECORD FOR LANCASHIRE CC

BATTING
First–class

	M	I	NO	RUNS	HS	AVGE	100	50
1987	2	1	0	37	37	37.50		
1988	6	9	2	216	64	30.85		2
1989	9	13	3	171	38	17.10		
1989 (Zim)	1	2	0	4	4	2.00		
1990	13	15	6	276	58	30.66		1
1991	12	16	4	315	101*	26.25	1	1
1992	8	10	2	230	115*	28.75	1	1
1993	2	3	0	31	20	10.33		
1994	11	16	1	386	50	25.73		1
1995	13	22	4	412	80*	22.88		1
1996 (Jam)	1	2	2	9	7*	0.00		
1996	10	12	3	437	95*	48.55		3
1997	17	25	4	825	95	39.28		8
1998	13	17	4	304	64	23.38		2
1999	5	8	2	125	45*	20.83		
2000	1	1	0	0	0	0.00		
Total	125	173	37	3778	115*	27.77	2	20

CENTURIES

101* v Yorkshire, Scarborough 1991
115* v Derbyshire, Blackpool 1992

BOWLING

First–class

	O	M	RUNS	WKTS	AVGE	BEST	5WL	10WM
1987	33.5	7	64	3	21.33	3–28		
1988	137.1	43	367	15	24.47	5–79	1	
1989 (Zim)	18	8	44	3	14.66	3–44		
1989	187.5	46	473	21	22.52	4–60		
1990	245.0	76	662	12	55.16	3–42		
1991	237.2	42	787	12	65.58	3–58		
1992	164.5	41	522	12	43.50	3–44		
1993	31.2	2	133	1	133.00	1–66		
1994	251.5	72	662	33	20.06	5–23	3	1
1995	363.4	111	889	35	25.40	4–50		
1996 (Jam)	14	3	35	1	35.00	1–35		
1996	223.4	64	645	22	29.31	5–116	1	
1997	448.4	131	1218	45	27.06	4–44		
1998	345.4	80	978	36	27.16	4–21		
1999	129	29	443	9	49.22	6–43	1	
2000	24	14	32	2	16.00	2–23		
Total	2855.3	769	7954	262	30.35	6–43	6	1